"It is almost beyond imagining that the Scouts should be under attack by such strong and well-established forces as assail them today. Scouting itself teaches us what to do in the face of that assault. As Winston Churchill said, "[Scouting] speaks to every heart its message of duty and honor: 'Be Prepared' to stand up faithfully for Right and Truth, however the winds may blow." This book by Hans Zeiger reminds us of this duty. Both the book and its author are a blessing."

Larry P. Arnn, President, Hillsdale College

"Hans Zeiger is America's most effective defender of Scouting. That is because he has lived Scouting, and his book tells it all."

Robert B. Carleson, Chairman, American Civil Rights Union

"Hans Zeiger is one of the most inspiring, articulate young voices for moral principle in America today. Hans possesses profound understanding of the most critical issues of our time—coupled with exceptional ability to rally others to worthy causes—and I am honored to commend his new book, Get Off My Honor, to all thoughtful Americans who care deeply about the moral preparation of our nation's youth. As Hans persuasively urges, we must save the noble tradition of the Boy Scouts, and to do this we must save Scouting from the radical agenda of those who are intent on destroying its very foundations—true manhood, fidelity to principle, and faith in God. The effort to save the Boy Scouts deserves everyone's support."

Ambassador Alan Keyes,
Chairman and Founder, Declaration Foundation

"In Get Off My Honor, Hans Zeiger pulls no punches and, like any good Eagle Scout, ties up all the loose ends. Weaving colorful, firsthand accounts amid well-documented chapters on the Scouts' history and recent trials, Mr. Zeiger paints a vivid picture of an American institution under attack, and equips readers so they can rise to the Scouts' defense. This is the most vital, honest book about Scouting out there."

Robert Knight, Author, The Age of Consent: The Rise of Relativism and the Corruption of Popular Culture; Director, Culture & Family Institute; Eagle Scout, Troop 80, Cape Elizabeth, ME

"Hans Zeiger has written an important book that gives a personal and insightful account of the significance of the Boy Scout movement to America and describes the critical battle to defend Scouting from the cowardly and despicable attacks being waged against it. It is a must-read for citizens concerned about the youth of our nation and the protection of traditional moral values."

Edwin Meese, Former Attorney General of the United States

"Hans Zeiger's book is a must-read for anyone concerned with the war on Scouting and, for that matter, the culture war currently engulfing America. He explains why and how some are determined to destroy the Scouts and provides ammunition for Scouting's defenders. If we are successful in defending them, Hans will deserve a fair share of the credit for that success."

Kirby Wilbur, Talk Show Host, 570KVI Seattle

GET OFF MY HONOR

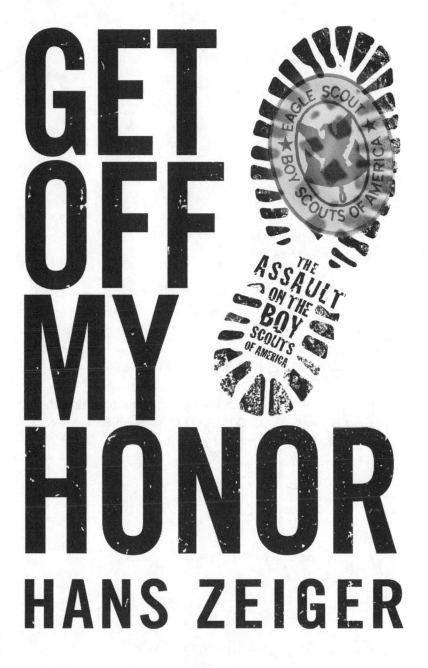

EAGLE SCOUT ★ ★ BOY SCOUTS OF AMERICA

THE ASSAULT ON THE BOY SCOUTS OF AMERICA

HANS ZEIGER

BROADMAN
&HOLMAN
PUBLISHERS

NASHVILLE, TENNESSEE

13-digit ISBN: 978-0-8054-3180-3
10-digit ISBN: 0-8054-3180-2

Published by Broadman & Holman Publishers,
Nashville, Tennessee

Dewey Decimal Classification: 369.43
Subject Heading: BOY SCOUTS \ DISCRIMINATION

1 2 3 4 5 6 7 8 9 10 09 08 07 06 05

Contents

This book is dedicated to the
world's best teacher, grandpa, and Boy Scout leader,
Ed,
and to his late wife, my grandma,
Wilma.

Foreword

These are strange times. We are a nation at war with a fierce and brutal adversary: terrorists who hate us for our faith, our freedoms, and our Judeo-Christian values—our very way of life. At the same time, we are also at war with ourselves—where faith, freedom, and Judeo-Christian values are under attack from fellow citizens who insist that we embrace their way of life, one that is antithetical to what most of us want for our children and their prospects.

We should have no doubt that we can ultimately prevail against that first foe. I have spent most of my life with the soldiers, sailors, airmen, Guardsmen, and Marines who defend us against violence from our adversaries. I'm confident that today's young Americans are sufficient to the task. It is the second antagonist, the opponent here at home, who presents a more precarious future. And no American institution embodies the nature of the trouble ahead more than the Boy Scouts of America (BSA).

As Hans Zeiger so carefully recounts in the pages that follow, the Boy Scouts of America—now nearly a hundred years old—are in the crosshairs of some of the wealthiest and most litigious and powerful opponents in the United States. Their goal is simple: to force this venerable organization to abandon its long-standing commitment to faith in God and what many of us euphemistically call traditional values.

What is it that has so engendered the wrath of the far left in this country? That, too, is clear-cut. Boy Scouts are required to adhere to a code of conduct. And just as they have for nearly a century, the Boy Scouts still challenge young boys—soon to be men—to something bigger than "self": to service for God and country. The

Boy Scout oath, or promise, that my father taught my brothers and me—and that I taught to my son—and that tens of millions of boys have mastered over the years is highly offensive to the radical left in this country:

On my honor I will do my best
To do my duty to God and country and to obey the Scout Law;
To help other people at all times;
To keep myself physically strong, mentally awake,
and morally straight.

What's so repugnant about that? Nothing—unless you are one who insists that there is no God; that nothing is bigger than "self"; that there are no limits to self-gratification; or that the term "morally straight" is offensive because it proscribes certain kinds of behavior, considered anathema in most cultures, but that you enjoy.

Those who contend that our entire society must accept their radical norms demand that the BSA abandon the "duty to God" and "morally straight" phrases in the Scout Oath and amend the Scout Law wherein boys commit to being:

Trustworthy, Loyal, Helpful, Friendly, Courteous,
Kind, Obedient, Cheerful, Thrifty, Brave, Clean, and Reverent

For most of us, those dozen virtues define the kind of man we would like our daughters to marry, the kind of employees we value, the boss we would like to have, and the kind of people we welcome as friends.

Secular radicals now assert that the BSA must not only drop the offending "duty to God" and "morally straight" phrases in the Oath but must also either revise or eliminate the definitions of "Clean" and "Reverent" or face the wrath of the courts.

The BSA handbook portrays "Clean" and "Reverent" as follows: "A Scout keeps his body and mind fit and clean. He goes around with those who believe in living by these same ideals. He helps keep his home and community clean." And, "A Scout is reverent toward God. He is faithful in his religious duties. He respects the beliefs of others."

Those terms sound fine to this former scout, son of a scout, brother of an eagle scout, father of a scout—and a former scout leader. They very likely resound favorably with most Americans. But to homosexual activists, the ACLU, atheists, and the legions of lawyers that they have retained, those are fighting words. According to them, the Boy Scouts of America will either have to drop these terms, radically amend them into meaninglessness, or be destroyed.

Unfortunately, the radical left has found sympathetic allies in so-called "public interest charities," in the courts, and in government bureaucracies from the municipal to the federal level:

- Despite evidence that Scout programs help to reduce teen crime and improve school attendance and graduation rates, municipal and state governments have banned Scouts from using publicly-owned facilities because the BSA insists that "morally straight" prevents practicing homosexuals from participating in the Scouts.

- Some regional United Way charities and major corporations no longer contribute to their local Scout Councils because of the BSA policy on homosexual activity.

- Connecticut officials have eliminated the Boy Scouts as a charity eligible to receive donations through the state employee payroll deduction plan because the BSA "discriminates against homosexuals."

- Military recruiters find that young men who come to them with a background in scouting generally have better mental, moral, and physical fitness than youngsters who have not. The Service Academies actually favor applicants who are Eagle Scouts. Yet, the Department of Defense has warned all U.S. military posts, bases, and stations against sponsoring Boy Scout troops because of a lawsuit brought by the ACLU that such support violates the "separation of church and state."

The result of this assault from the radical left has been a significant reduction in contributions—and diminished opportunity for American boys. The judges who find the phrase "one nation under God" offensive in the Pledge of Allegiance to our flag are equally affronted by "duty to God" in the Boy Scout Oath and

"Reverent" in the Scout Law. Apparently the patriotism of the Boy Scouts offends some Americans. Reverence for God in Scouting evidently angers others.

"In God We Trust" is our national motto, not a right-wing, political slogan. We adopted it because those who forged this nation trusted God. If it's good enough for our coins and currency, why isn't it OK for America's boys?

Hans Zeiger has chronicled all of this and more in *Get Off My Honor: The Assault on the Boy Scouts of America*. He not only exposes the agenda of the radical left but offers prescriptions as well. This is a valuable work for every parent and community in a nation that should be concerned about the kind of young men we will have in the future.

Critics of Scouting, those who claim that in the twenty-first century such an organization is anachronistic—that it's no longer relevant—need to read this book as well. And while they peruse its pages they should consider this:

A few years ago in another part of the world, a handful of men with a charismatic leader took a group of boys aside and spent years teaching them evil, to hate, how to kill others, and how to kill themselves. On September 11, 2001, nineteen of those young men boarded four airliners here in the United States and killed 2,797 people.

Contrast what those nineteen young men had been taught with the lessons an American boy learns from positive role models as a Boy Scout.

Is Boy Scouting still important to America? It is if you believe that young men should be taught about respect for others, respect for self, and about the sanctity of human life. It is if you want young men to use their God-given gifts and talents to better themselves and their community. And it is if you want this nation to continue to be "the land of the free and the home of the brave."

Oliver L. North
LtCol USMC (Ret.)

Acknowledgments

Whatever problems there may be with the book may be blamed on the sixteen-year-old who decided to write it. On the other hand, if it is worth reading, some people who are mostly older and smarter than I deserve some praise.

Before I understood how to get a book published, I sent amateurish promotional letters to a handful of pro-family groups around the country, and I was honored that Phyllis Schlafly took the time to write back a brief note of encouragement. I also was inspired and helped along the way by Peter LaBarbera of the Illinois Family Institute, Robert Carleson of the Scouting Legal Defense Fund, Gary Yinger of the Eagle Scout Rally for Truth Foundation, Gavin Grooms of Save Our Scouts, WorldNetDaily's Joseph Farah and Tom Ambrose, and Scouting professional Britt Vincent. Thanks to Colonel Oliver North for the foreword.

For the early history of the Boy Scouts of America, David Macleod's research was most valuable. Even more appreciated was Dr. Macleod's feedback on the second chapter.

Many thanks to the wonderful people of Broadman and Holman Publishers. My literary agent Mark Gilroy was a blessing for a first-time author.

Thanks to my parents, Kim and Walt, and to my brothers and sisters. Thanks to my dad for feedback on the manuscript.

I owe acknowledgment to my Boy Scout leaders whose selfless devotion to character and community is ever underappreciated: Doug, Tom, Ernie, Mike, Cameron, Dick, and several others. Finally, this book is dedicated to my grandparents, Ed and Wilma. Grandma—a quiet and graceful and supportive woman—died last year, and Grandpa—an energetic and practical and good man—is still Scouting after half a century.

And, to God be the glory.

Introduction

Cultural critics of the Boy Scouts say the Scouts are odd and antiquated with their uncool brown uniforms, teaching useless knot tying in a technological world, their indoctrination of survival skills in a convenient world, occasional retreats to the backwoods in a civilized world, and ceremonial recital of character creeds and honor codes in a world that long ago rejected moral absolutes.

I would not be one to dispute Scouting's outmodedness by modern standards. As recently as 2005, I went to google.com to search for my own beloved Troop 174, and I found no trace of it on the entire World Wide Web.

Still, something is deeply attractive about a slice of a community's existence in which boys get together and do the same things in the same ways their fathers and grandfathers did. The next generation of Americans exists on a perilous, unspiritual diet of change and instability. Young people desperately need permanent things to understand life and grow into responsible, respectful citizens.

While Troop 174 may not be noted by the Internet age, it's a permanent institution for boys between eleven and eighteen years old.

I still recall entering that age during my eleventh birthday party in February 1996. My mother invited various family members to join us for a casual family celebration at a local Japanese restaurant. Today, I've forgotten everything about that party except a question that came from my grandpa after dinner: "So, Hans, when are you going to join the Scout troop?" Age eleven, after all, meant I was eligible to join.

I hadn't really considered the question previously, or perhaps I had hid it at the back of my mind for fear a bear or rattlesnake might someday get the best of me on a backwoods wilderness trail.

But there was more meaning to the question than I realized at the time. And of all people who understand what it means to be a Boy Scout, my grandpa, Ed Zeiger, does.

He was a Scout in the early 1940s when the Great Depression was merging into World War II. A member of a somewhat inactive troop, he rose through the ranks to Life Scout along with his twin brother, Bill. Grandpa likes to say that he learned more as a Boy Scout and a newspaper deliverer than he did in school.

During his seventy-six years, my grandpa has accumulated a rack full of hats. He grew up with dust streets and a one-room schoolhouse in Kittitas, Washington, where he learned about hard work and how to reuse, repair, and restore. My grandpa likes to save things, from money to old car parts. He doesn't buy things he doesn't need in the first place, and he is a seasoned veteran at finding uses for parts to fix his legendary cars when they need repair. My grandpa holds on to his hats, too, because he may need them for something else someday. He remains active in serving other people, relying heavily on the life skills he has picked up over the years.

He speaks in third-grade classrooms about what life was like during the 1930s and makes frequent visits to the new elementary school named in his honor, where he recently coordinated a school talent show. He is a former teacher and elementary school principal, a Kiwanian, choir member, church elder, basketball player, die-hard University of Washington Huskies fan, the father of seven and grandfather of thirty, and a Boy Scout leader.

My grandpa has worked with hundreds of Boy Scouts in Troop 174 as an assistant Scoutmaster since he came, with my grandma, Wilma, to the once-small farming town of Puyallup, Washington, to begin his teaching career and start a family in 1952.

Occasionally, at a Troop 174 court of honor, my grandpa will acknowledge the days a boy has accumulated in hiking and camping. But I doubt anyone has ever calculated the number of days and nights my grandpa has been out on the trail—they would figure in the years instead of days.

When I joined him for a trip to Boy Scout Camp Hahobas every summer and winter during my teenage years, I counted on routine storytelling. "At this bend in the road," recited my grandpa, "is where we used to turn off toward the lower drive along Hood Canal to get to camp." Even though it was the same story as last time, it was worth hearing again.

He's the kind of person who has learned to enjoy life, but he never turns on the television to do so. He says he likes to be a part of the real thing.

And so, I sat opening my birthday gifts that evening in 1996, listening to my grandpa ask me if I would join the real thing.

AFTER IGNORING the question for three months, I finally showed up at a troop meeting one spring evening at the historic Troop 174 Scout house. A wild game of Six Square was in process in the middle of the floor. Intimidated by the apparent skill required to properly activate the Six Square ball and remain in the game, I busied myself along a far wall looking at a row of oversized bulletin boards featuring a half century of troop photography. One bulletin board displayed black and white photos of the troop in its early days. A World War II veteran named George Newcomer founded Troop 174 in 1951. The troop met in a local elementary school down the road from Mr. Newcomer's house before he decided to have the troop renovate and move into a chicken coop behind his house. Today, the walls of the abandoned chicken coop still stand a foot from the southern wall of the current Scout house—a grand affair constructed of plywood and other cheap materials and consisting of a large meeting hall, a small back conference room, two storage rooms, and a tiny bathroom, which was built in the early 1960s.

At the front of the Scout house was a large redbrick fireplace, the mantle of which was covered in various Scout trinkets, each odd and end with a story that my grandpa would be capable of telling on a moment's notice. There was a cooking pan with a gaping hole in the bottom, an old toilet lid taken from a rotting Kibo seat that collapsed one week at Camp Hahobas, a mysterious painted rock, a Tomahawk from Philmont Scout Ranch in New Mexico, a model rocket, and a small Norman Rockwell Scout print on a wooden backing.

Above the fireplace was a wall painting of Mount Rainier and the words "Troop 174." Below were three small wooden desks labeled Senior Patrol Leader, Assistant Senior Patrol Leader, and Scribe, each desk graffitied with the names of its previous occupants.

Lining a far side of the wall was a plenteous stack of heavy-duty wooden crates filled with everything needed to set up the troop's own Walla Lee campground at Camp Hahobas—from cooking utensils and pots and pans to tarps and rope. Nearly fifty mounted certificates containing the words "Official Charter: Boy Scouts of America" purchased a corner above a table stacked with monthly *Boys' Life* magazines, the official membership publication of the BSA, dating to the late 1960s.

The senior patrol leader soon called the meeting to order. "To-night," started Ben while Scouts shuffled to straighten their uniforms and apply tree-bark clasps to their yellow Troop 174 neckerchiefs, "we'll have Brad lead us in the Scout oath."

Brad, my cousin only a month older, joined the Scouts on his eleventh birthday with a bit more enthusiasm than I had at the same milestone. He and I spent our time in Scouts together to a great extent, but I managed to beat him in the race to Eagle Scout.

Brad began the oath with his Scout salute high in the air, facing the Troop 174 flag. A vast array of official annual BSA ribbons recognizing the troop for another year of existence bedecked the troop flagpole. The others joined in with Brad. "On my honor, I will do my best to do my duty to God and my country, and to obey the Scout law, to help other people at all times, to keep myself physically strong, mentally awake, and morally straight."

Through the meeting, I learned about earning the Scout rank: "repeat the Pledge of Allegiance," "demonstrate the Scout salute, sign, and handclasp," "show how to tie a square knot," and "understand and agree to live by the Scout oath, the Scout law, the Scout motto ('Be Prepared'), the Scout slogan ('Do a good turn daily'), and the Outdoor Code ('As an American, I will do my best to be clean in my outdoor manners, be careful with fire, be considerate in the outdoors, and be conservation minded')." I busied myself with these matters until the end of the meeting when Ben called, "Fall in!"

My grandpa approached the middle of the room with a small, old book in his hand. "Signs up," he said briskly. Everyone in the room stopped talking as three-finger salutes rose in echelon. Ed put his hand down and said, "Scoutmaster minute." My grandpa generally shared troop authority with the official Scoutmaster, Doug.

"Tonight I want to read you a passage from the original Boy Scout handbook," Ed said. "This is from the chapter entitled, 'Scoutcraft.'"

He began. "'In all ages there have been scouts, the place of the scout being on the danger line of the army or at the outposts, protecting those of his company who confide in his care.

"'They had to know how to live so as to keep healthy and strong, to face danger that came their way, and to help one another. . . .'"

And so Ed continued, then concluded his reading, "'Wherever there have been heroes, there have been scouts; and to be a scout means to be prepared to do the right thing at the right moment, no matter what the consequences may be.'"[1]

He paused a moment, closed the book, and prompted, "Circle up."

With that, all the Scouts stood and formed a circle. Each Scout crossed arms and held hands with the Scouts on either side of him. To the tune of "O Tannenbaum," they sang:

Softly falls the light of day
As our campfire fades away
Silently each Scout should ask:
Have I done my daily task?
Have I kept my honor bright?
Can I guiltless sleep tonight?
Have I done, and have I dared
Everything to be prepared?

After the vespers concluded, everyone unlinked arms and made a Scout salute into the center of the circle. "May the Great God above us be with us until we meet again."

Hands dropped in unison and the circle dispersed. Scouts headed for the door or stayed to discuss tenting arrangements for the upcoming hike.

Before leaving with my dad, I was given an extra Boy Scout handbook. I took it home that evening and began to acquaint myself with Scouting.

Eventually, I decided to stick with it. Five short years after I joined Boy Scout Troop 174, I became an Eagle Scout. In the process I became a man. And I learned about the importance of character, friendship, survival, and honor.

When my grandpa presented me the Eagle Scout badge with his customary emotion showing boldly, he read the Eagle Scout charge: "The foremost responsibility of the Eagle Scout is to live with honor. To an Eagle Scout, honor is the foundation of all character. He knows that 'a scout is trustworthy' is the very first point of the scout law for good reason. An Eagle Scout lives honorably, not only because honor is important to him, but because of the vital significance of the example he sets for other scouts. Living honorably reflects credit on his home, his church, his troop, and his community."[2]

On a wall in the old Scout house is a hand-drawn mural featuring several dozen names of Eagle Scouts dating back half a century. My name is among them.

Shortly after I became an Eagle Scout in June 2001, I began work on this book because I took to heart the words of the Eagle Scout charge, and I realized that a Scout's honor is under attack in American culture. Honor, "the foundation of all character," has been nearly forgotten by a generation of Americans who, as products of a morally relativistic culture, care more about serving themselves than about their obligations to the community, the nation, and the world. Character itself has gone by the wayside.

Mine is a unique generation of Americans. We have enjoyed the fruits of innovation, freedom, and prosperity. But children are often faced with the challenge of being divided between two parents who broke their marriage vows. In the midst of the chaos, cultural forces are working on the minds and hearts of young America.

The most visible assault on contemporary childhood in America is waged by persuasive messages of the mass media. My generation is influenced by the popular culture of MTV, magazines, radio, and the Internet. Punk rockers and rappers make a living from the antifamily rhetoric they spew in the form of jumbled words and a beat. At various points in my growing up, the cultural heroes of my peers have included Dennis Rodman, Britney Spears, Justin Timberlake, and Eminem. Pleasantries, manners, and etiquette have been replaced with profanity, rudeness, and rashness.

About the resulting decadence of the next generation, James Q. Wilson wrote, "We are not entitled to be surprised. If we set several million teenagers free from direct parental or market supervision, knowing that a fraction of them lack a strong moral compass; if we expect those young people to learn from what they see about them; and if what they hear is a glorification of the virtues of individualism and self-fulfillment, then we ought to be thankful that any adolescents are left intact."[3]

Many kids today are intact, like most kids in my Scout troop, but many others reflect a culture that rejects character.

Consider the boy who is twelve years old today. He is the right age for recruitment into his local Boy Scout troop, and he is the right age to become prey to a radical anticharacter movement that sweeps our culture.

He enjoys surfing the Internet, but his innocent mind is vulnerable to a sudden pop-up ad that contains X-rated material. He enjoys watching television, but the programs include such waste as *South Park* and *The Simpsons*. He goes to a public school paid for by taxpayers, but he cannot learn about the role of God in history and science. He is just beginning to enter adolescence, but his school and the popular media exploit sexuality all around him.

He was born in 1992, a year of a record number of illegitimate pregnancies. Thirty-two percent of all children born that year were born out of wedlock.[4] And in 1993, Dr. Thomas Lickona of the Center for the Fourth and Fifth Rs (Respect and Responsibility) released a report in which he noted ten trends in the ethical conditions of youth: rising violence, increased cheating, growing disrespect for authority, cruelty to peers, resurgence of bigotry in schools, a decline in the work ethic, sexual precocity, growing self-centeredness and declining civic responsibility, increase in self-destructive behavior, and "ethical illiteracy" or a poor understanding of core virtues.[5] According to Michael Medved, "In every corner of contemporary culture childhood innocence is under assault. . . . Society seems perversely determined to frighten and corrupt its own young in a misguided effort to 'prepare' them for a harsh, dangerous future."[6]

The Boy Scouts is all about preparing today's twelve-year-old boy for life. But unlike preparing for the harsh and dangerous future of modern culture, the Boy Scout handbook says, "Be prepared . . . to live happily and without regret, knowing that you have done your best."[7]

Therein lies the Boy Scout difference. It is not the goal of Scouting to prepare for harshness and danger that accompany a life without character or courage. Scouting prepares for hope and determination, not fear and cowardice. When a Scout is truly prepared, he is not oblivious to the harsh and the dangerous because he monitors it closely. And he fights it where it invades his community and his nation.

WHEN JOHN WAYNE was nearing death in 1979, he made one of his final public appearances at a fund-raising banquet for the dedication of the John Wayne Outpost Camp in Los Angeles. Those are "nice words," he said of the Scout law. "Trouble is, we learn them so young we sometimes don't get all the understanding that goes with them. I take care of that in my family. As each boy reaches Scout age, I make sure he learns the Scout law. Then I break it down for him, with a few things I have picked up in more than half a century since I learned it."[8]

Then, the dying legend explained:

Trustworthy—The badge of honesty. Having it lets you look at any man in the eye. Lacking it, he won't look back. Keep this one at the top of your list.

Loyal—The very word is life itself; for without loyalty we have no love of person or country.

Helpful—Part sharing, part caring. By helping each other, we help ourselves; not to mention mankind. Be always full of help—the dying man's last words.

Friendly—Brotherhood is part of that word. You can take it in a lot of directions—and do—but make sure and start with brotherhood.

Courteous—Allow each person his human dignity; which means a lot more than saying, "Yes, ma'am" and "Thank you, sir." It reflects an attitude that later in life you wish you had honored more . . . earlier in life. Save yourself that problem. Do it now.

Kind—This one word would stop wars and erase hatreds. But it's like your bicycle, it's just no good unless you get out and use it.

Obedient—Starts at home. Practice it in your family. Enlarge it in your friends. Share it with humanity.

Cheerful—Anyone can put on a happy face when the going is good. The secret is to wear it as a mask for your problems. It might surprise you how many others do the same thing.

Thrifty—Means a lot more than putting pennies away; and it is the opposite of cheap. Common sense covers it just about as well as anything.

Brave—You don't have to fight to be brave. Millions of good, fine, decent folks show more bravery than heavyweight champs just by getting out of bed every morning, going out to do a good day's work, and living the best life they know how against the law of odds. Keep the word handy every day of your life.

Clean—Soap and water helps a lot on the outside. But it is the inside that counts, and don't ever forget it.

Reverent—Believe in anything that you want to believe in, but keep God at the top of it. With Him, life can be a beautiful experience. Without Him, you are just biding time.[9]

But the reality is that despite the Boy Scouts' good influence on society, much of society is determined to destroy the Boy Scouts instead of promote them. Today, Hollywood and the rest of popular culture have changed their attitudes toward the Boy Scouts. Peter

Applebome wrote, "Now when Scouting shows up in popular culture it's often as an arch or campy effort in mockery like the February 2000 issue of *Out* magazine which features on the cover a too-pretty Scout with thick lips and a pink sleeveless Scout shirt."[10]

Contrast the attitudes of John Wayne and film director Steven Spielberg, who started in cinema by filming his Scout troop in the 1960s. Spielberg sat on the board of advisers for the national Boy Scouts of America (BSA) beginning in the early 1990s. But on April 17, 2001, Spielberg announced his resignation from the board, stating, "The last few years in Scouting have deeply saddened me to the Boy Scouts of America publicly participating in discrimination. It's a real shame."[11]

I will not deny that the Boy Scouts participate in discrimination. Though the Scout law is a positive code ("A Scout is" as opposed to "Thou shalt not"), discrimination is thoroughly implied.

Veteran media analyst Mary Mostert noted a Scout discriminates against lying by being trustworthy, against disloyalty by being loyal, against selfishness by being helpful, against hate by being friendly, against rudeness by being courteous, against cruelty by being kind, against disobedience by being obedient, against complaining by being cheerful, against financial irresponsibility by being thrifty, against cowardice by being brave, against filth by being clean, and against ungodliness by being reverent.[12]

If a Scout declares himself incapable or unwilling to do his best to do his duty, he is no more a Scout than a rat is an eagle.

AS A TWENTY-YEAR-OLD Eagle Scout, my life is a small fraction of my grandpa's. But I am nevertheless an Eagle Scout who sees the challenge of this generation in asserting the rights of free association and preserving moral character.

When I am a grandfather, I want to carry on the same proud tradition my grandpa gave to my father and his brothers and to me, my brothers, and cousins. Though my grandpa's commitment to Scouting is far beyond what I'll ever be able to accomplish, I want my children and grandchildren to be able to go to a Boy Scout meeting or a camping trip to learn the importance of character. If at all possible, I want to stay around Puyallup and guide my own children through Boy Scout Troop 174.

But in the meantime, I have a few words for those who'd like to destroy the Boy Scouts. If necessary, I'll spend my life defending the values of the Boy Scouts; and if the current condition of the culture war is an indicator, it looks as if I'm committed for good.

CHAPTER 1

★★

America Needs the Boy Scouts

When eighty-four-year-old Erling Olsen's pacemaker quit in 2002, his family wondered how much longer he had to live. They asked if he wanted anything in life that he didn't get. He said yes—as a youth, he had earned the rank of Eagle Scout, but he never got the award.

In the summer of 1933, Olsen had completed all of the requirements for Eagle Scout, baking and serving for a Depression breadline as his Eagle project. He waited for a friend to finish the Eagle requisites so the two buddies could have their court of honor together. Sadly, Olsen's friend died that summer, and Olsen moved on from Scouting.

He began a small garbage collection business at the age of sixteen, and at age seventeen became a deckhand on a ship bound for Norway. He returned to his native Washington State, got married in 1940, attended the University of Washington, and joined the Army Reserve Officer Training Corps. When World War II broke out, Olsen joined the U.S. Navy and served his country.[1] After the war, he worked as a commercial fisher and ran small businesses in Seattle and on the Olympic Peninsula. He and his wife settled in Port Angeles, Washington, and raised two children.[2]

Olsen's son Tom told the *Bremerton Sun* that his father had maintained a collection of eagles throughout his life. Erling Olsen longed to join what Eagle Scouts call the Eagle's nest. In February 2003,

Erling "Bub" Olsen became the oldest recipient of the Eagle Scout award in the ninety-three-year history of the Boy Scouts of America.

Like any Eagle Scout candidate, Olsen went before a board of review to be interviewed and to share his experience in Scouting and life in general. Unlike other Eagle Scout candidates, Olsen had a mountain of experiences in honor, character, and duty. "'It was quite a different experience from any other [Board of Review] I've done,' Chief Seattle Boy Scout Council advancement chairman Allen Anderson said. 'Usually we wonder what the boy will do for his community, because an Eagle Scout is a leadership position. With Bub, we asked what he's done for the past 70 years. He had quite a list.'"[3]

Father. Veteran. Entrepreneur. Sailor. Grandfather. And at long last, Erling Olsen joined the legendary nest.

I called Olsen shortly after he was awarded the distinguished badge to interview him for a column I was writing for the *Seattle Times*. I was curious about his outlook on the past, present, and future of Scouting. Speaking to Olsen, I gained a greater appreciation for my own Eagle Scout award. The value of the Eagle Scout designation is as high today as it was ninety-three years ago when the Boy Scouts were founded.

"The Boy Scouts of today is better than when I was in the Scouts," Olsen said, referring to well-established programs and troops that have access to resources and volunteers like never before.[4]

Still, according to Olsen, the Scout oath and law are exactly the same as they were when he was a Scout in the 1930s. Of course, in the ideas of liberal modernity, something that's the same today as it was seven, eight, or nine decades ago is probably politically incorrect, male-dominated, and based on absolute truths. Such are the Boy Scouts of America.

And such are the reasons for opposition to the Scouts in the culture wars. It is common knowledge that the Boy Scouts of America prohibit homosexuals, atheists, and females. Around the country, the Boy Scouts are under increasing pressure to become politically correct, watered-down, feminized, and secularized. Inevitably, these changes would come at the expense of such virtues as duty to God, moral cleanliness, bravery, and reverence.

But for Olsen, the issues are simple. "Religion should be there. People who don't want it, shouldn't be in it [Scouting]." And homosexuality: "If you admit it, I don't think you should be in it [Scouts]."[5]

TO A NEW GENERATION steeped in the doctrine that personal preferences are irrelevant to anyone except the person who holds them, Olsen's views may seem antiquated. But if ideas have consequences, we might conclude that faith and values have impact on the present and the future, that an entire culture is subject to the choices of the individuals who compose it. The Boy Scouts have always believed that by turning boys into men of character, society will be better.

Instead of being applauded, the Boy Scouts are protested, boycotted, and sued. The Scouts' position in the mainstream civic community is on the decline, and it is increasingly drawn into the heat of controversy. What *Newsweek* magazine called "the struggle for the soul of the Boy Scouts" truly represents the larger war between right and wrong, between honor and cowardice.

The battle for the Boy Scouts must be fought on two fronts. First, the Boy Scouts must be defended because they have the civil right to be a voluntary association irrespective of the winds of public opinion or the trends of political correctness. Second, the Boy Scouts must be defended because they are good. In his 1937 book *Great Contemporaries,* Winston Churchill wrote, "[The Boy Scout Movement] speaks to every heart its message of duty and honour: 'Be Prepared' to stand up faithfully for Right and Truth, however the winds may blow."[6]

Today, the capacity of the Boy Scouts to stand for principle and character is vulnerable. The shots fired at America's finest youth organization are no longer only frivolous lawsuits filed by girls. Charitable funding is being severed. School boards and city councils are telling Scout troops they can no longer meet on public premises. Churches and community organizations have declared enmity with the Scouts.

Take the Eagle Scout badge as an example of what's happening to the Boy Scouts' reputation. I went through the ranks of Scouting, told that the Eagle rank was a sure qualifier for a host of decent jobs. Of course, that's true in many ways, but Peter Applebome pointed out, "In the enlightened corridors of liberal America, attaining Eagle may be seen more as a sign of retrograde dweebdom than as having the right stuff."[7] For some employers in "liberal America," considering the job application of an Eagle Scout is more a reason to consider referral to a diversity trainer than to add to the payroll.

The Boy Scouts' reputation has suffered greatly from a declining portrayal in the mainstream media. When editorialists write of the Scouts and television news films them, the label is often homophobic, bigoted, chauvinist, militaristic zealots.

IN JUNE 2003, the *Philadelphia Daily News* published an editorial asking, "What's the difference between the Taliban and the Boy Scouts?" Any decent newspaper with the interest to ask such a question would be quick to point out the differences, and the differences are stark. But not the *Daily News*. The editorial stated, "We can't help being disturbed by similarities between the Afghan fundamentalist group and the homophobic American shapers of youth."[8]

The following week, the *Daily News* had the audacity to repeat and defend its outrageous comments from the previous week.[9]

At issue was the Philadelphia Cradle of Liberty Boy Scout Council's renewal of a commitment to exclusive membership standards. The local United Way had dropped funding from the Scouts in Philadelphia, and the Pew Charitable Trust had announced that it would not give a promised $100,000 to the council.[10] The Philadelphia City Council made initial moves toward ejecting the Scouts from a headquarters at Twenty-second and Winter streets given to them "in perpetuity" in 1929.[11]

If the division between moral paradigms is inevitable in America, the Boy Scouts must accept the challenges. In Philadelphia, supporters can take away funding. The city can seize the seventy-five-year-old headquarters building. The Scouts can survive without it.

But don't dare touch my sacred honor. And don't ever liken me to the Taliban because I'm involved in the Boy Scouts.

Don't ever put the Boy Scouts who fought in World War I, World War II, Korea, Vietnam, Afghanistan, and Iraq in the same category as the men who hijacked planes and flew them into the World Trade Center and the Pentagon on September 11. Don't ever say the Boy Scouts of America are a purveyor of terror and hatred.

Every adult Boy Scout leader I've met is a practicing believer in tolerance. That isn't to say there aren't bad people who go into Scouting; there are, and the Boy Scouts of America have a procedure for preventing and removing poor role models from leadership. Yet the Boy Scouts worked on the issue of inclusiveness long before it was the buzzword of the day.

AFTER THE FORMATION of the Boy Scouts of America in 1910, a thirty-four-year-old attorney and children's advocate named James E. West was asked to be the chief Scout executive. West developed his passion for leadership development in children and young adults because as an orphan growing up he had been handicapped, spending two years in a hospital. He assisted in organizing the Child Rescue League, a group dedicated to placing children in decent foster homes. He inspired Theodore Roosevelt to organize the 1909 White House Conference on Dependent Children.[12] And after graduating from law school, West established the nation's first juvenile court.[13]

In the words of one author, "He had great energy, flinty will, little charm, much insecurity, and a mania for efficiency."[14] Thus, West was a perfect fit for leading the Boy Scouts, and he served as executive secretary for nearly thirty-three years. In large part, West established the mission of leadership for which Scouting has come to be known. In the October 1923 edition of *Boys' Life,* West wrote: "America needs leaders who have come up through the ranks. It is doubly to the credit of the boy who sticks in school in spite of handicaps, whether because of lack of money, poor health, or other causes. If any boy is struggling with this problem and wants personal help, please write to me. I will gladly do what I can to help reason the matter out."[15]

Having grown up disabled, West was dedicated to facilitating the needs of disadvantaged children and minorities. West's sympathy for diverse backgrounds and needs was rooted in his belief that each individual is worthy of respect. He believed in extending equal opportunity to all boys who affirmed the Scout oath and law.

Today, more than one hundred thousand Cub Scouts, Boy Scouts, and Venturers with disabilities are registered in the organization. The Boy Scouts accommodate a wide array of disabilities in their advancement programs. The Boy Scout handbook is printed in a braille edition for blind Scouts, and each merit badge pamphlet has been recorded on cassette tape. Closed-captioned training videos have been produced for deaf Scouts. Beginning in 1965, the BSA waived the maximum Scout membership age of eighteen for individuals with mental retardation. Today, thousands of Scouts with mental, physical, and emotional disabilities are given opportunities to learn basic skills, reach for goals, and cooperate with other children and adults.

According to a pamphlet written by the Council Services Division of the Boy Scouts, the program for Scouts with disabilities focuses on two objectives. First, the program aims to help unit leaders develop an awareness of disabled people. Second, it encourages the inclusion of Scouts with disabilities in Cub Scout packs, Boy Scout troops, Varsity Scout teams, Venturing crews, and Sea Scout ships. Some Scout troops have been formed exclusively for the purpose of meeting the needs of disabled children. Special all-blind and all-deaf troops are active in America's communities.

In 1981, BSA launched the disabilities awareness merit badge. Revised in 1993, this badge fosters an appreciation for the contributions disabled people bring to a community and encourages Scouts to do their good turn for those with disabilities.[16] According to the Boy Scout handbook: "While they might have special ways of overcoming certain conditions, people with disabilities are full members of our communities. They often have much to offer. Be sensitive to their needs, but then look beyond their limitations and get to know them as the people they really are."[17] Far from being a terrorist organization as the *Philadelphia Daily News* alleges, the Boy Scouts teach respect for those in the community who are different.

Most local councils develop an advisory commission to establish programs that accommodate the needs of disabled Scouts. Since August 1977, national Scout Jamborees have included an educational trail for disability awareness. Many local councils have built similar trails.[18] In advancement, disabled boys cannot cheat; they cannot use their disability as an advantage over others. However, if a Scout is wheelchair-bound and cannot swim, those requirements may be waived. If a Scout cannot use his legs to hike ten miles, he may travel that distance in his wheelchair.

IN THE BOY SCOUTS, every boy who is willing to affirm Scout principles and to "act as a Scout at all times" has a place. "Scouts come from all walks of life and are exposed to diversity in Scouting that they may not otherwise experience. The Boy Scouts of America aims to allow youth to live and learn as children and enjoy Scouting without immersing them in the politics of the day. We hope that our supporters will continue to value the Boy Scouts of America's respect for diversity and the positive impact Scouting has on young people's lives. We realize that not every individual nor organization prescribes to the same beliefs that the BSA does, but we hope that all Americans can be as respectful of our beliefs as we are of theirs and support the overall good Scouting does in American communities."[19]

It is not merely a position that the BSA promotes when public pressure is on, it has been advocated, instilled, and pushed since Scouting began in 1910. Journalist Heather MacDonald wrote, "Long before diversity trainers appeared to browbeat America, the Scout Law urbanely commanded boys to 'respect the convictions of others in matters of custom and religion.'"[20]

African Americans were a part of Scouting even in its early days. In Camden, New Jersey, a black preacher founded a church troop in the 1920s and recruited members so successfully that one in five local Scouts was black.[21] Though troops were segregated in the South until the 1920s and '30s[22], more than five hundred Scouts belonged to black troops in Louisville, Kentucky, in the 1920s and an advisory council of community leaders was formed to support the troops.[23] According to David Macleod, segregation was not enough to stop fellowship between Scouts of different races. In the South, some white boys helped black friends on the Boy Scout requirements and handed down old uniforms.[24]

A Cuban American named Mario Castro on April 4, 2000, was welcomed into the Boy Scouts of America as the 100-millionth member. The twelve-year-old from Brooklyn, New York, immigrated to the United States from Mexico City with his family when he was two years old. Now, Mario is learning about the essence of the American spirit as he works and plays in Boy Scout Troop 986, chartered to Saint Michael's Roman Catholic Church in Brooklyn. Mario is an excellent example of how the Boy Scouts mold the lives of young racial minorities.[25] One BSA outreach called Scouting Vale la Pena! (It's worth the effort) targets Hispanic American youth like Mario Castro.[26]

Scouting has always been associated with the promotion of American Indian cultures and skills. A founder of American Scouting, Ernest Thompson Seton, had originally started the Woodcraft Indians to teach American Indian skills and lore to boys. Many of the outdoor skills a Scout learns come from American Indian tradition, and Scouting is quick to acknowledge the influence of that heritage. A popular merit badge is Indian lore.

In 1956, the Boy Scouts and Girl Scouts together established the American Indian Scouting Association (AISA) to help adult troop leaders become familiar with Native American cultures and customs. It also educates Scouts about the importance of American Indians and facilitates special programs such as a professional-quality Indian dance group sponsored by one Colorado Scout troop.[27]

BSA uses other outreach programs to expand membership while spreading strong character and leadership. In many neighborhoods across America, poverty, crime, and family disintegration are tragically defining factors in the lives of youth. The opportunities to become involved in an organization like Scouting are limited. At the other end of the spectrum, 25 percent of children grow up in a rural setting where poverty is also common and access to major American institutions is limited. For both rural and urban youth, the Boy Scouts have developed an outreach program called Scoutreach. It recruits adult leaders who volunteer their time in an underprivileged area where the cultural and financial situation is often challenging. The BSA assists with funding such endeavors and trains Scout leaders to cope with the difficulties of volunteering in an urban or rural setting.[28]

One Boy Scout historian wrote that the character builder movement of the early 1900s arose from concern for helping lower-class boys. "Essentially, [character builders] represented an attempt by the dominant middle classes to rescue and impose good order on what seemed the vulnerable and potentially the most dangerous section of the lower classes."[29]

Heather MacDonald profiled a Harlem inner-city Scout troop in 2000 in *City Journal* magazine: "Though scouting arose in response to a perceived moral crisis in youth nearly 100 years ago, its founders could not possibly have foreseen how much more desperately their gift to poor, drifting, boys would be needed today. Indeed, Scouting is a brilliant method for infusing children with a set of values that can be especially hard to find in the inner city. The little details that fill each meeting constantly reinforce a code of conduct based on self-restraint, neatness, and courtesy—the essentials of civilized life."

Among inner-city youth, the constant search for moral order often ends in gang participation, drug use, violence, and worst of all, hopelessness. But the Scouts offer positive influence, a sense of belonging, and hope for the future. "Inner city boys are starving for discipline; Scouting allows them to follow and to lead," wrote MacDonald.

While a culture war of one type is raging through America's inner cities, Scouting remains a ray of hope where it exists. MacDonald wrote, "The traditional values of Scouting are shriveling up everywhere today; in troubled neighborhoods, they are a precious balm." And one of the most important advantages of Scout troops

in the inner cities is offering positive male influence to young disadvantaged boys, many without fathers. "For many ghetto parents,
Scouting's greatest boon is the Scoutmaster. . . . The Scoutmaster
may be the only stable adult in a child's life."

According to MacDonald, Scouting gives disadvantaged youth a
sense of belonging in the community and a sense of love for country.
"Cultivating a love of country in disadvantaged boys is a cure for
alienation; it centers them in an identity far larger and more valuable
than race or class and assures them that this is their country, too."[30]
In the Boy Scouts millions of young boys—rich and poor, popular
and socially inept, black and white, Protestant and Catholic—have
cast their gaze on a cause higher than mere self-interest.

WILL ROGERS OBSERVED, "The problem with Boy Scouts is
that there isn't enough of them." He was correct. If the term Boy
Scout can be synonymous with excellence, there is a deficit of Boy
Scouts indeed.

A survey by Louis Harris and Associates in the late 1990s tracked
the academic and social outcome of Boy Scouts and Boy Scout alumni
and showed that Boy Scouts with five years or more in the program
outpace their non-Scout peers by far in a variety of categories. Boy
Scouts were less likely to be involved in criminal behavior and less
likely to use drugs or to be addicted to alcohol. While 98 percent of
Boy Scouts graduated from high school, only 83 percent of the general peer population received a diploma. Boy Scout college graduation
rates were 40 percent compared to only 16 percent for others. Furthermore, Boy Scouts were more likely to hold a student leadership
role in high school and college, more empathetic to the needs of other
people, more capable of making hard moral choices, and more likely
to respect the ecosystem. Perhaps most interesting is that the income
level of former Boy Scouts was greater than that of their peers. Thirty-
three percent of former Scouts earned more than $55,000, while that
could be said of only 17 percent of non-Scouts surveyed.[31]

But accomplishments are only valuable for society if they are
founded on high moral character. "Character is destiny," said
Heraclitus.

When former McDonnell-Douglas CEO Sanford McDonnell set out to improve the operations of his company, he started by changing his company's code of ethics. "We had a code of conduct as all organizations have, a 'thou shalt not' code; but we didn't have a positive 'thou shalt' code of ethics. So I gave a task force the Scout Law and told them that I didn't want the McDonnell-Douglas Code to read like the Scout Law, but I did want it to cover the twelve points of that law." Beginning in 1983, McDonnell-Douglas executives set up a standard eight-hour training program to teach the employees about their Scout law-based code.[32]

Character comes before success, and the Boy Scouts—past and present—are living proof of that.

Many of our nation's military leaders, politicians, business executives, scientists, explorers, and innovators have been Boy Scouts, and many are Eagle Scouts.

Boy Scouts are taught to achieve, to make an impact in the world, and to inspire others to do the same. In 1973, fifteen-year-old Michael Herrara of Miami did something no other Scout has ever done. He earned every merit badge possible, for a total of 118. The Associated Press reported, "The more common badges came easy, but cotton farming took some initiative. And snow skiing in Miami was a long shot at best."[33] From the ranks of Scouting have sprung some of the most amazing success stories, the most stunning rescues, and the most diverse and useful life skills for millions of boys and young men for more than ninety years.

THE BOY SCOUTS of America have a good mission—rooted in the strength of the American family and embraced by churches, schools, and civic organizations. It is a mission to pass on to each succeeding generation of young American men the preparedness necessary for the preservation of the ideals that give strength to our nation. Among a host of youth organizations, the Boy Scouts stand apart by an unwavering commitment to the development of character and leadership in young men.

In an age when morality is often viewed as irrelevant to culture, the Boy Scouts of America have remained firm as a driving force of values and ideals. Scouting is able to involve boys in meaningful experiences that challenge leadership, test character, and initiate manhood. Scouting has no cultural agenda or political cause to speak of. It does have a clear sense of honor that transcends the passage of generations.

Yet the challenges to the Scout oath and law are more severe than ever before. Instead of calmly passing great principles and life skills from generation to generation, the Boy Scouts now find themselves in the midst of a great moral war. The Boy Scouts must contend against a legion of cultural forces molding young men in a radically different direction from Scouting.

TRAGICALLY, THE POINT has come at which the Boy Scouts have begun to consider—in local councils in major cities—giving in.

In 2000, the chief executive officers in nine major councils—New York, Los Angeles, West Los Angeles, Chicago, San Francisco, Philadelphia, Minneapolis, Boston, and Orange County—wrote letters requesting that the Boy Scouts of America change the membership policy to include homosexuals.[34] During summer 2001, executives from those nine councils met to discuss ways to balance pressure to compromise against the national BSA policy with the Boy Scout national council itself. One Scout executive in the Greater New York Council called the Boy Scouts national leadership, based in Irving, Texas, "A bunch of rednecks from Texas."[35] Council executives in San Jose, California; Narragansett, Rhode Island; and Saint Paul, Minnesota, also have requested the Boy Scouts of America lift the ban on homosexuals.[36] By 2002, twenty-five Boy Scout councils requested that the national organization allow local chapters to set their own policies regarding homosexual membership.[37]

In Florida in 2001, the Dade Boy Scout Council was threatened with a termination of $1.5 million in funding from the local United Way, and a group called Safeguarding American Values for Everyone (SAVE) lobbied the council to give up the homosexual ban. In response, the council cut its own funding from public sources, ceased recruiting efforts in public schools, and developed

a sensitivity/diversity training program for adult leaders to effectively deal with homosexual youth. The new program included a
partnership with Project Yes, a Miami-based operation that educates the public about the needs of homosexual youth. According to conservative activist and 2000 presidential candidate Gary
Bauer, the decision in Dade "may be the Boy Scouts' Waterloo."[38]

The nation's smallest Scout council, Piedmont, near San Francisco, defied the Boy Scouts of America policy on homosexuals directly. The Greater New York Council also made an inconspicuous
rebellion against the BSA prohibition on homosexuals by crafting
a nondiscrimination code that stated, "Prejudice, intolerance and
discrimination in any form are unacceptable."[39]

In spring 2002, the Massachusetts Minutemen Council in
Boston, a council comprising 330 troops with 18,000 young men
in America's Patriot State, agreed to adopt a "don't ask, don't tell"
policy that ignored sexual morality and cleanliness instead of condemning homosexual behavior. At the Minutemen Council annual
fund-raising dinner in May 2002, major contributors representing
business and nonprofit organizations gathered in Boston, and the
event seemed more like the banquet for Scouting for All than the
Boy Scouts of America. The council invited Boston area homosexual
radio talk-show host David Brudnoy to be the master of ceremonies
and asked Brudnoy to unveil a new diversity merit badge.[40]

But Philadelphia's Cradle of Liberty Boy Scout Council has had
the worst of it. During the 2003 Boy Scouts of America National
Convention in Philadelphia, the council announced it would be
admitting homosexuals, and within days, eighteen-year-old Scout
camp counselor Greg Lattera came out as a homosexual.[41] Besides
giving in to the United Way and left-wing activist groups, the Cradle
of Liberty Council gave up on its 87,000 members who joined an
exclusive organization for the sake of exclusivity. Those eleven- and
twelve-year-old boys knew when they joined their troops that not
everyone can be a Boy Scout. Only those Scouts who do their best
to do their duty to God and country, to obey the Scout law, to help
other people at all times, to keep themselves physically strong, mentally awake, and morally straight are worthy of the Boy Scout title.

Philadelphia's outright rejection of Scout policies did not settle well at the national convention, and the Philadelphia Scouts were quickly forced to reaffirm national BSA policies or forfeit their charter. The name calling spurred by the *Philadelphia Daily News,* mentioned earlier, was a result of the Cradle of Liberty Council's preserved charter.

The milder reforms instituted by the councils of Dade in Florida, Piedmont, Boston, New York City, and elsewhere are seemingly justified on the insistence that the new policies are simply an effort to update the Boy Scouts for changing times, times in which "diversity" must be tolerated, accepted, and celebrated in all of its forms: natural, cultural, and moral.

But unlike diversity, which, contrary to popular belief, is not a moral virtue, honor requires a Scout's allegiance to a code of conduct, and that means neither homosexuals nor atheists can become leaders or members of the Boy Scouts.

If "intolerance" is the synonym for honor in the lexicon of political correctness, may it be said that the Boy Scouts are intolerant of dishonesty, disloyalty, treason, impurity, disobedience, wastefulness, ignorance, indifference, hopelessness, and bondage.

And if intolerance of moral slavery is of any worth to the men who lead the councils in Philadelphia, Piedmont, Boston, Dade, New York, and elsewhere that are challenging the Boy Scouts of America for being too politically incorrect, may they, before it is too late, consider that their decision to abridge a sacred honor is like a vote for moral slavery.

WHAT'S THE DIFFERENCE between the Boy Scouts—the real Boy Scouts, that is, who, in Churchill's phrase, stand up for "right and truth however the winds may blow" and never give in—and the Taliban?

Trustworthy. Loyal. Helpful. Friendly. Courteous. Kind. Obedient. Cheerful. Thrifty. Brave. Clean. Reverent.

Such qualities will defeat the Taliban and other great evils of our time.

CHAPTER 2

★★★

A History
of the Boy Scouts

Chicago Ledger publisher William D. Boyce went to London in
1909 to secure his arrangements for the African Balloonograph
Expedition. On his way to a business meeting, he became disori-
ented in the dense London fog. He stood on the curb of a crowded
street, looking around frantically to determine his whereabouts.

"'I was in doubt whether to try to cross the street when a boy
about ten or twelve years old, I think he had a lantern or a light of
some type in his hand, asked me if I wished to cross the street,' re-
called Boyce. 'I told him I did, and he piloted me to the other side.
I then offered to tip him and he refused it on the basis that he was
doing a good turn as a Boy Scout.'"

His curiosity piqued by the young Boy Scout's uncommon
kindness, Boyce completed his preparations for the African safari
and made his way to the London headquarters of the Boy Scouts.
In the office of the legendary Lord Robert S. Baden-Powell, Boyce
gathered as much information and literature he could about this
new youth movement.

During his four-month hot-air balloon safari, Boyce remained
captivated by his collection of brochures, booklets, and articles
about Baden-Powell's Boy Scouts. Boyce discovered a new dream
while out of the country: "'I thought—what a wonderful thing it
would be for our American boys.'"[1]

THE BOY SCOUTS of America were founded during the mid-point of a great revolution. Between 1860 and 1960, wrote James Q. Wilson, social opinion changed from advocating self-control to endorsing self-expression.[2] The halfway point between the two years was, of course, 1910. American Scouting began that year as an effort to restore self-control to the lives of America's young men.

For most boys in the late nineteenth century, school, church, and employment occupied most of their time. But in the early twentieth century, an increasingly accepted Darwinian view of the world gave place to a revolutionary social invention: adolescence. G. Stanley Hall's two-volume *Adolescence* appeared in 1904, and the new ideas of adolescence endured throughout the past century.[3]

Before the twentieth century, childhood and adulthood had been the only stages of life. Adolescence was "hardly a threatening social invention," according to Wilson. But combined with "the ethos of radical individualism and commitment to self-expression of educated elites," adolescence was "troubling."[4] The Progressives lobbied to prohibit child labor and advocated the Social Gospel in churches. Young people became unemployed and alienated from religion and traditional social life.

Thus, for many young people growing up in the early 1900s, free time and an abundance of recreation opportunities were fresh phenomena. But, as one early Boy Scout leader observed, "School provides leadership for only about one thousand of the five thousand hours a year a boy has for activity."[5] And in their newfound liberty of free time, young men were increasingly mischievous.

William Forbush's 1901 book *The Boy Problem* reflects this American problem.[6] Recreation movement leader Henry S. Curtis criticized rural boys for learning to "smoke cigarettes, to shoot craps, [and] to tell smutty stories."[7] Ernest Thompson Seton, founder of the Woodcraft Indians, blamed urbanization, industrialization, and the rise of spectator sports for turning "such a large proportion of our robust, manly, self-reliant boyhood into a lot of flat-chested cigarette smokers with shaky nerves and doubtful vitality."[8]

Schools were of higher academic quality than ever before, but they failed to teach morality. Dr. James Russell, a professor of education at Columbia University and an early supporter of the Scouting movement, noted that "the state seems to have overlooked the fact that intellectual power is as great an asset to the crook as to the honest man."[9]

The character development movement arose to remedy the boy problem. Its leaders hailed from a wide array of backgrounds and ideologies. Progressives sought reform and new institutions. From this, a recreation movement emerged to respond to the surplus of free time among boys, and many schools began to sponsor extracurricular activities and sports for the first time. William Forbush began summer camps for boys to "develop those savage virtues which are the admiration of boyhood."[10] Most high schools did not have basketball and football teams until the 1910s.[11] Conservatives also joined the character builders, seeking to preserve Victorian moral tradition in a rapidly changing world. And "rugged individualists," such as Theodore Roosevelt, found new opportunities to combine the adventurous, the manly, and the good in young men. In the words of David Macleod, professor of history at Central Michigan University and author of *Building Character in the American Boy,* "Strength merged with virtue in the Victorian association of physical health with moral virtue."[12]

Character developers recommended that boys become more well rounded and civilized. When he became physical education director of the YMCA in 1886, Luther Gulick geared the organization to combine physical hardiness with Christian morality.[13] But as the boy problem worsened, even Gulick realized that the YMCA was insufficient to address the growing social problems.

IN ENGLAND, where the boy problem had been just as much a challenge, Baden-Powell founded the international Scouting movement in 1907. Born to a prosperous family in 1857, Baden-Powell was only three years old when his father died, and his strong-willed mother raised him. Young Robert spent much of his time roaming the woods and developed a passion for the outdoors. He joined

the army and trained in mechanical drilling, then did reconnais-
sance work in South Africa. At various times, Baden-Powell was either working with or fighting among native people in West Africa
and in India. When he was given command of his own regiment,
Baden-Powell trained men he described as "without strength of
character [or] . . . resourcefulness" to become self-reliant scouts.[14]

Baden-Powell led troops in the Boer War in South Africa and
became a national hero for his wartime feats. On his return to England, he criticized his country's lack of military readiness. According to Michael Rosenthal, the Boer War had "seemed to announce"
England's depressing "moral, physical and military weakness."[15]
Sir Frederick Maurice's report on military readiness showed that
during the Boer War, three-fifths of British men were unprepared
for military service.[16]

Baden-Powell soon learned England's problem: Young men
lacked the motivation and sense of purpose to fight for their country. After being asked by the Boys' Brigade to inspect parades,
Baden-Powell found the incessant parading and drilling boring
and unproductive. While he began his work in character development with the intention of making the organization more practical, Brigade leaders did not share Baden-Powell's agenda.[17]

So Baden-Powell struck out on his own, relying on his own
capital of fame and heroism to fill a market for character development that was unmet or at the least had been attempted in the wrong
way. Baden-Powell was just as critical of modernity and the state of
boyhood and manhood as his contemporaries in America. "With its
town life, buses, hot and cold water laid on, everything done for you,"
he wrote, society tends to "make men soft and feckless."[18]

In 1907, Baden-Powell published leaflets promoting his new
vision for character development; his objectives included discipline, observation, health, patriotism, chivalry, lifesaving, and
woodcraft, an idea somewhat adapted from Ernest Thompson
Seton's Woodcraft Indians in America.[19] In fact, wrote Peter Applebome, "Part of Baden-Powell's genius was to steal from everyone,
to put together a movement that was nature and militarism, world
peace and national preparedness, fun and serious, left and right,

an alluring mix of disparate elements—British explorers and Zulu tribesmen, the garish triumphs of Empire and the quiet glories of the woods."[20] Baden-Powell set to work to distribute his leaflet, raise money, and interest adult men in forming units.[21]

Within only a few months, Baden-Powell organized the first Boy Scout camp at Brownsea Island, a dramatic event featuring legendary campfire tales of war and adventure by the master himself, B. P., as he was known.[22] The famous initials became the inspiration for the Scout motto, "Be Prepared," and Baden-Powell introduced the Scout law as a positive guide for character traits.[23]

Baden-Powell marketed the Scouts to potential supporters by expressing his concerns for social unrest motivated by class differences. And he stressed the importance of preparing the British Empire for military strength. "Our business is not merely to keep up smart 'show' troops," he declared, "but to pass as many boys through our character factory as we possibly can; at the same time, the longer the grind that we can give them the better men they will be in the end."[24] Baden-Powell's Scouting movement was not "just an organization a boy joined," wrote Michael Rosenthal, "but a total ideology that he absorbed and that thereafter determined his thinking, feeling, and acting."[25]

Baden-Powell's *Scouting for Boys* was the B. P. guidebook on how to live and succeed. It discussed patriotism, conservation, etiquette, marksmanship, camping, and, of course, character. *Scouting for Boys* became an instant best-seller and through its reprintings and revisions, made Baden-Powell, with the exception of Shakespeare, the most widely read British writer of all time.[26]

THE TWO MOST important forerunners of the Boy Scouts of America, besides Scouting in Great Britain, were the Woodcraft Indians and the Sons of Daniel Boone.

Naturalist and magazine illustrator Ernest Thompson Seton founded Woodcraft Indians in 1902 as a camping experience for adolescent boys at his Connecticut estate. Dissatisfied with the strictness of his own upbringing and the alienation of his father, Seton sought to give hope to young men.

There were two purposes of Woodcraft Indians. First, Seton wanted to instill in boys the Indian value of ecological conservation, and, second, wanted them to enjoy recreation in "the spirit of the Indian religion." But Woodcraft Indians was poorly organized and lacked moral content and practicality.

With similar motives, Daniel Carter Beard, an illustrator and freelance writer, founded Sons of Daniel Boone in 1905 to boost subscriptions to *Recreation Magazine*. Sons of Daniel Boone emphasized pioneering and patriotism, and Beard described it as "essentially American. We play American games and learn to emulate our great American forebears in lofty aims and iron characters." Like the Woodcraft Indians, Sons of Daniel Boone lacked structure and stability. Clubs founded with excitement and anticipation were short-lived.[27]

Shortly after the founding of the Boy Scouts in Great Britain, American character developers began a race to begin the Boy Scouts of America. First, E. M. Robinson of the YMCA made Baden-Powell's *Scouting for Boys* available to young members while laying plans to build the Boy Scouts of America as a community-service wing of the YMCA. At the same time, Hearst Newspapers was strategizing about how to use the idea of Scouting as a circulation gimmick. *Harper's Weekly,* William Verbeck's Military School, and a few other organizations also had their eyes set on the future BSA.

But William Boyce beat everyone to the punch by incorporating the Boy Scouts immediately after he returned from his African balloon trip in 1910. Boyce even began lobbying members of Congress for a congressional charter to jump-start the organization. But Boyce was "lost" in the fog when it came to leading the Boy Scouts, and he welcomed the YMCA's enthusiastic good turn for getting the BSA off the ground.

In June 1910, Robinson called together a meeting of America's most influential character developers at the YMCA headquarters in New York City. Leaders of the Red Cross, Big Brothers, *Outlook* magazine, and public school athletic leagues and others conferred and elected the Boy Scouts of America committee. Ernest Thompson Seton was elected chairman, and committee members included Robinson, recreation advocate Luther Gulick (founder of the modern playground), photographer and antipoverty activist Jacob Riis, Daniel Carter Beard, and Republican Party leader and banker Colin Livingstone.

The committee began raising money, recruiting leaders, and writing articles, and Seton nearly plagiarized Baden-Powell's book to make an American version of the Boy Scout handbook. Five hundred thousand copies of the book were published with the sponsorship of Minute Tapioca. Within only three months, Baden-Powell came to visit the United States, a move perceived by the founders of the BSA as the official christening of American Scouting.

But with Seton at the reins, insufficient organization and structure became a problem for recruitment, and momentum faded. The BSA founding committee turned to the Sage Foundation for new funding and hired the young attorney James West as executive secretary to oversee the growth of American Scouting.[28]

When West arrived at the YMCA offices in New York in January 1911 to take the helm, he established three committees—Code, Badge, and Organization—to determine the most effective program. The Code Committee, led by Dr. Jeremiah Jenks, drafted and approved the Scout oath and law.[29] With major changes to the British version emphasizing American reliance on codified virtues, David Macleod wrote, the Americans added "Mosaic import" to the oath and law.[30]

For several years, West and his growing staff traveled the country, recruiting and training council and troop leaders. By 1922, membership had grown to nearly 433,000.[31] The more the program developed, the more exclusive it became. The more exclusive it became, the more distinguished became the title of Boy Scout, and Eagle Scout in particular. West was unwilling to compromise on the standards required to attain the ranks and merit badges of Scouting. West compared his standards to a Harvard diploma.[32]

When it came to certain aspects of Progressivism, the public schools lagged behind the Boy Scouts. When the changing economy spurred demands for vocational training, the Boy Scouts rose to satisfy a challenge unmet by schools. Addressing teachers in 1916, James West pledged that his organization would put a bold emphasis on career development.[33]

But vocational training in the Boy Scouts, as with any Scout activity, was secondary to character development. *Scouting Magazine* wrote in the early days that "a Boy Scout must grow up 'free' from every blemish and stain. . . . Only then will he be fully equipped to . . . fight the battles of business life."[34]

The Boy Scouts quickly acquired esteem in communities across America. The Boy Scouts first emerged with a national good turn during World War I in 1917 when they unveiled a new promotional slogan: "Help Win the War." With armistice the following year, the slogan became "The War Is Over, but Our Work Is Not." Indeed, the Scouts performed countless hours of national service both during and after the war, when membership topped four hundred thousand and a national influenza epidemic broke out.[35]

Robert MacDonald wrote: "The Scout movement was a success because it answered so many hopes and anxieties; it was both 'progressive' and reactionary, responding, on the one hand, to a number of liberal ideas in education and social theory, and, on the other, to a wide range of conservative, imperialist, and militarist opinion."[36]

NOT LONG AFTER the founding of the Boy Scouts of America, leading intellectual attitudes about adolescence changed radically.

Apparently, the Boy Scouts, along with the Girl Scouts, filled the market niche for youth character development, and the character development movement itself seemed to disappear within the decade. James Q. Wilson reported, in 1890, 1900, and 1910, one-third of childrearing articles published in *Ladies Home Journal, Women's Home Companion,* and *Good Housekeeping* had been on the subject of character development. But by 1920, only 3 percent of childrearing articles in the three magazines surveyed dealt with character development. The new fad that replaced it was "personality development."[37]

Personality development came from the psychology field. The shift from character development to personality development marked the beginning of what Charles Sykes called "the triumph of the therapeutic." Instead of pursuing traditional instillation of character for the young, psychological personality development filled a "vacuum created by the decline of institutional faith and the collapse of the moral order it has provoked," and "psycho-analysis has assumed many of the functions traditionally performed by religion."[38]

In the 1930s and 1940s, all America endured the hardships of the Great Depression and World War II. Boy Scouts helped on the home front with the war effort, and many Scouts went to war themselves.

American Scouting expanded its membership and became known internationally for an emphasis on character and mastery of the outdoors. Two important branches of Scouting—the Sea Scouts for aspiring sailors and the Explorer Scouts for vocational education—were founded in the 1930s.[39] The first national Jamboree was held in 1937 in Washington, D.C., with more than 27,000 Boy Scouts participating out of a total membership of 1,129,841; the next Jamboree was held in 1950 at Valley Forge, Pennsylvania, with 47,163 Scouts and leaders attending of 2,795,222 total members.[40]

When Scout executives decided to expand programs to younger boys in 1930, they had no idea that by 1956, Cub Scout membership would surpass Boy Scout membership. Even today, Cub Scouts remain the majority in Scouting.

Seeking expansion, the Scouts opened membership in the Explorer Scouts to females in 1968. Criticized for having an old-fashioned, unpractical program, Scouting executives rewrote the Boy Scout handbook in 1972 to emphasize urban skills and modern lifestyles while nonchalantly attempting to diminish the importance of camping and the outdoors.[41]

With its attempt at a new, modern look and initial rejection of select Boy Scout traditions, Boy Scout membership dropped drastically by the late 1970s.[42] Despite its efforts to the contrary,

Scouting became known more than ever as an antiquated corps of campers who wore outmoded uniforms, tied useless knots, and sang old-fashioned campfire songs. Realizing that its image was in the decline, Scout executives adopted an advertising slogan that emphasized this desperation: "Scouting today's a lot more than you think."[43]

After coming to grips with reality, Scout executives decided to stick with the popular, traditional Scouting program. William Hillcourt was hired to author the 1979 Boy Scout handbook, returning the focus to Scout tradition and the outdoors.[44] Within a short period of time, Boy Scout membership stabilized.[45]

But by this time, the Boy Scouts were at odds with an unfriendly new cultural elite. Given the inevitable clash between the new elite and Scouting's traditional values, the BSA braced itself, beginning in the late 1970s, for the impending culture wars. The Boy Scouts of America took the motto, "Be prepared," to heart.

CHAPTER 3

★★

A Defense
of Honor

On a warm September evening following summer vacation, Troop 174 reconvenes for the fall court of honor. On this occasion the various badges and patches earned at summer camp are bestowed on Scouts, ranks conferred, summer jokes reiterated, and anecdotes and adventures of the fifty-mile hike told.

The court of honor is a formal occasion. Full uniforms are expected. The senior patrol leader serves as master of ceremonies, and he calls the event to order with the pledge of allegiance, followed by the words, "Would all Scouts and former Scouts please remain standing?"

Fathers and sons stand together with the three-finger Scout salute held high as mothers sit and observe the lighting of candles to signify the Scout oath and law. One candle in the middle is lit first: "This candle represents Scout spirit," says the senior patrol leader. Then, one by one, the other candles are lit until the room is illuminated with the twelve candles representing the law and the three candles representing the oath.

In the opening of a Boy Scout court of honor, one witnesses how Scouting holds character in high esteem. What is important for the critics of Scouting to understand is that the Scout oath and law are not suggestions. They are codes of honor a Scout is sworn to uphold, a fact that may complicate the spurious theory that the principles of Scouting are changeable by the whims of morally relative modern culture.

The court of honor celebrates the old synthesis of character we call honor. An individual has honor when he is able to find purpose and meaning in things beyond himself and devotes his entire being to those things. A Scout has honor when he honors the right things: God, country, family, and neighborhood.

SINCE THE 1960s at the latest, many corners of American culture have moved beyond the absolutes expressed in the Scout oath and law toward the shifting values of radical individualism. "Contemporary society," wrote sociologist Robert Nisbet, "tends by its very structure to produce the alienated, the disenchanted, the rootless, and the neurotic."[1] Instead of fostering self-sufficiency, radical individualism has, according to Nisbet, "resulted in masses of normless, unattached, insecure individuals who lose even the capacity for independent, creative living."[2] While the rugged individualist Baden-Powell demanded that "a boy should take his own line rather than be carried along by herd persuasion," radical individualism is the lethal combination of selfishness with dependency and a herd mentality.[3] Today, personal selfishness in its most vile strains has been projected into society at large.

The counterculture of the 1960s—what became the dominant culture of today—was engineered by a generation of young people unsatisfied with America's old restraints of tradition, religion, family, and moral absolutes. A life of service to God and country seemed quite dull in the minds of the new cultural elite. Individual rights, privileges, feelings, desires, and conveniences seemed of far greater import than obligations, responsibilities, faith, courage, and self-sacrifice.

The concept of adolescence introduced only half a century earlier on the eve of the founding of the Boy Scouts was in the 1960s exploited to the extent that youth was no longer the rebellious age of society but the driving force against which all tradition and family and faith would become the new rebels. Charles Sykes contended, "Perhaps we might choose to envision the 'youth culture' not as a culture of young people but as a culture that refuses to grow up. . . . A culture that disdains the processes of self-control and restraint, celebrates impulse and immediate gratification, and insists upon the unlimited indulgences of its eccentricities will always have a soft spot for adolescence."[4]

Given the contrast between the Boy Scouts' virtue-concentrated worldview and the new morally relative, individualistic youth culture of the sixties, "the 1960s counter-culture and the Boy Scouts of America were a train-wreck waiting to happen," wrote Heather MacDonald. "Here was a supremely patriotic service- and family-oriented institution suddenly up against a movement celebrating rebellion and declaring 'AmeriKKKa' a fascist regime."[5] And if, as Charles Sykes argued, the sixties youth culture was and is a culture "that refuses to grow up," the contrast with Scouting could not be more clear. For it is precisely the purpose of Scouting to guide boys in the growing-up process.

The 1968 annual report of the Boy Scouts of America expressed alarm at the rise of crime, drug use, and "the impractical flower world of the Hippie." Scouting, the report said, was a "positive force to capture the attention and interest of youth."[6] While Scouting had once been a "symbol of the nation's shared values and virtues," wrote Peter Applebome, "the consensus frayed in the 1960s and 70s," and "Scouting's role became more complicated."[7]

To summarize the complexities of what happened to American culture during and since the sixties, it could be said that a radical paradigm shift occurred. Today, instead of seeing a single, unified culture in which the family, church, school, government, and markets work together toward common goals, we are, in the words of Gertrude Himmelfarb, "one nation, two cultures."[8] The American society that embraced Norman Rockwell's picturesque Boy Scouts is a thing of the past.

A societal breakdown is what happens when social norms give way to unrestrained personal preferences, and individualism triumphs over community. We see the results of radical individualism and the breakdown of traditional community all around

us, when the United Way gives money to homosexual organizations but not to the Boy Scouts; when schools and cities and states
pass nondiscrimination codes in favor of gays and lesbians and
atheists and agnostics but deliberately discriminate against the
Boy Scouts of America; when churches disregard biblical statements about homosexuality in hope that they might broaden their
church membership to homosexuals, even if it means canceling
a charter with the Boy Scouts; when a newspaper likens the Boy
Scouts to the Taliban while caring deeply for the rights of cap-
tured Taliban fighters as they await trial as prisoners of war in
Guantanamo Bay, Cuba.

IN TODAY'S divided culture, it is difficult for the Boy Scouts to
avoid compromise while the politically correct elite so adamantly
demands it. Heather MacDonald wrote, "The elites in the press,
the universities, and the chattering professions, having thoroughly
absorbed the adversarial values of the 1960s, have kept the scouts
from regaining their place in the American imagination."[9]

Critics of the Scouts contend that the BSA can regain a more
hallowed place in the American mind by simply falling in line
with the rest of American mainstream civic culture, by allowing
homosexuals and atheists to become members. Dr. Jay Mechling
proposed that "perhaps we can set aside the morality/immorality
question as inappropriate for an institution the likes of the Boy
Scouts."[10]

In opposing atheists and homosexuals as members, the Boy
Scouts find themselves increasingly separated from mainstream
civic organizations that at one point or another have decided that
moral virtue, sexual preference, and religious belief are irrelevant
matters.

BUT THE BOY SCOUTS are doing a better turn for all of America
than they may have intended in the first place by sticking to principle. By standing firm in favor of traditional community standards
and family values, the Boy Scouts have become a living refutation
to the prevailing spirit of radical individualism.

Radical individualism celebrates self-esteem, the exaltation of self above all other priorities. "The self-esteem influence has so pervaded our culture that it is no longer perceived as anything but the most acceptable way of thinking," wrote theologian Jay Adams.[11] But there is something superficial about the doctrine of self-esteem espoused from the mainstream pulpits, motivational conferences, self-help books, and classrooms of today. Sociologist Frank Hearn wrote, "One may have the right to self-esteem or feeling good, though this is doubtful, but being good—being in a way that permits one to realize institutional goals—is an achievement. One earns self-respect only through the disciplined work of performing institutional duties or achieving institutional ideals."[12] While the culture of radical individualism espouses the notion that one should feel good regardless of whether he really is good or not, the Boy Scouts teach that one should only feel good once he has done his best to do his duty.

In all my dealings and studies of the Boy Scouts, I've never encountered the word "self-esteem" coming from the Scouts themselves. Adams said such neglect is perfectly justified. "There is no need for concern about how to love one's self, for so long as one seeks first to love God and his neighbor in a biblical fashion, all proper self-concern will appear as a by-product."[13]

It follows then that for a Boy Scout, rightful, deserved self-esteem is a natural benefit of character and of duty. But in that case, the esteem in question is less of a good feeling about self and more of a good feeling about God, country, and community. Honor is not merely about ego. Admiral Charles Larson wrote, "Sometimes moral courage does not result in awards or adulation, but one always earns pride and self-respect through uncompromising integrity."[14] Harvard government professor Sharon R. Krause said "There is something intrinsically admirable in the ambitious desire to live up to a principled code of conduct, in seeking self-respect on principled ground."[15]

When one does his best to do his duty, when one does a good turn daily, when one is prepared for the challenges of life, he won't keep his focus on self-esteem. Instead, he must be willing to face up to the harsh and demanding sacrifices that true service requires. If he is going to do his good turn daily, he must not focus on his own feelings but on the needs of other people. If he is going to be prepared, he must train his intellect on learning and his hands on working. And if, at the end of the day, a Boy Scout feels good about himself, it will be because he sacrificed and labored for it. Because he did not let the harsh burdens of life get him down. Because he had the character and selfless determination of a Boy Scout.

And that is precisely what is meant when the Boy Scouts speak of honor. Honor, it turns out, is the most poignant and desperately needed antidote to the self-esteem movement and its parent ideology, radical individualism.

Honor is a word frequently used and seldom understood. Even the Scout oath seems too simple to teach much about the meaning of honor. But the oath contains several great insights into honor: *On my honor, I will do my best to do my duty* . . .

First, honor is an individual possession: *my* honor. Honor is not collective, nor is it attributed to anyone other than the Scout who swears by it. Second, honor is the basis for action. In the oath, honor is a noun, and it is considered a foundation on which to exercise character. Third, honor is an absolute necessity for duty.

Krause defined honor as "the quality of character that makes one wish to live up to certain rules of conduct, a particular desire to uphold a general obligation."[16] Alexis de Tocqueville, a French political philosopher, defined honor as "that particular rule, founded on a particular state, with the aid of which a people distributes blame or praise."[17]

Honor is cultivated within communities and organizations that compose the culture. The culture—its ideas, customs, symbols, and heritage—causes individuals to find for themselves a higher calling, a purpose connected to the culture. "Culture," said Philip Rieff, "is another name for a design of motives directing the self outward, toward those communal purposes in which alone the self can be realized and satisfied."[18]

Wherever cultural institutions flourish in civil society, honor is cultivated. According to Tocqueville, "Every time men are gathered in a particular society, an honor is immediately established among them, that is to say, a set of their own opinions about what one ought to praise or blame; and these particular rules always have their source in the special habits and special interests of the association."[19] In other words, honor is simply a binding attachment to a code of character and a way of life developed and defined within an organization (a family, a church, or a nation).

Honor means that a person is willing to fight and even die to maintain his allegiances and to do so rightly. For an American soldier at war, honor is contingent on his ability to obey his superiors and serve his comrades. For the mayor of a town, honor is his capacity to serve the best interests of his neighbors. And for a Scout, honor has everything to do with the great code of ethics set forth in the Scout oath and law. Honor is carefully defined by the principles of the codes of Scouting, and honor is compromised by any whose character falls short of meeting those principles.

Honor is not only required for the identity of a private community organization like the Boy Scouts, it is also necessary for the very survival and advancement of a nation. Tocqueville wrote, "The more exceptional the position of a society is, the greater in number are its special needs, and the more the notions of its honor, which correspond to its needs, increase."[20] Since America is a great nation, America needs great men of honor.

But finding great men of honor is a challenging task in a democratic nation, Tocqueville observed. He believed that the dissimilarities and inequalities of men created honor and some men can be greater than others. But democracy works with great vigor toward equality that, at its extreme, precludes one man from becoming greater than another. Tocqueville warned that the acceleration of equality in a democratic society was a great threat to honor. In an aristocratic nation, he wrote, inequality lays the foundations for a natural type of honor where class and kin regulate one's sense of duty. But, he concluded that honor "is weakened insofar as these differences are effaced, and it should disappear with them."[21]

The reason honor did not disappear in America, Tocqueville reasoned, is that voluntary organizations and societies, families, and churches abounded and thrived. "The law of honor exists," he said of America, "but it often lacks interpreters."[22] As Tocqueville explained throughout *Democracy in America,* the search for interpreters of honor is an endeavor that takes place in and among the institutions of civil society.

Of course, voluntary associations like the Boy Scouts and churches cannot hold a monopoly on the people; while they work to impact the culture, they remain, after all, voluntary associations. Thus, "in a democratic nation like the American people, where ranks are confused and where the entire society forms a single mass, all the elements of which are analogous without being entirely alike, one can never agree in advance on exactly what is permitted and forbidden by honor."[23]

Nevertheless, voluntary associations are, in a sense, more than voluntary when they function correctly as a part of the civil society. If an individual is to be a part of society, he must at some point make a decision to associate with others who share his faith, ideas, or interests. Frank Hearn wrote, "Institutions embody collective codes of honor and discipline that guide the pursuit of institutional ideals or goods by specifying virtues—the dispositions and character traits—that enable people to undertake the honorable, disciplined, and difficult tasks necessary for the achievement of institutional goods. Institutions thus define the types of virtues, practices, and achievements that are honorable and worthy."[24] In the midst of inevitable confusion about honor, Scouting has effectively become what Tocqueville would call an interpreter of honor because, as an enduring institution, Scouting has made honor central to its mission.

Since Scouting is not exclusively concerned with its own internal affairs, it draws boys in and teaches them their connection to the larger community, nation, and world. As long as it has existed, Scouting has helped America at large to define honor for itself.

Democratic society and government can survive for a while without honor. But eventually, when times get tough, a nation must either revive its sense of honor or reject its own existence. "While most of the time liberal democracy can get by with good citizens, occasionally it needs great ones," noted Sharon Krause. "The heroic qualities at the heart of honor answer to this need: high and principled ambition, courage, pride, and the powerful desires for self-respect and public distinction."[25]

WHAT TOCQUEVILLE said about the desire of democratic peoples for equality is certainly a reality in America today. For the past several decades, we have witnessed an insatiable push toward greater equality. One need only examine the antidiscrimination codes to understand the extent to which equality has been pursued. "Such and such city or school or employer," the codes say, "will not discriminate on the basis of race, ethnicity, gender, sexual orientation, gender identity, language, veteran status, weight, height, age, hair color, financial status, and so on."

Equality is a good thing when it comes to political franchise and civil rights. "All men are created equal," proclaims the Declaration of Independence. During the Civil War and the civil rights movement of the 1960s, great men and women championed man's God-given equality of opportunity.

But throughout the course of the past few decades, equality has taken on a new dimension. Instead of a movement toward equal rights of opportunity—the right to the "pursuit of happiness" and such—minority groups have made a loud cry for an inalienable right to absolute equality of condition.

An entirely new vocabulary accompanies this push. Words like *discrimination, tolerance, multiculturalism,* and *diversity* appear with great regularity in the literature of bureaucrats, legislators, company executives, educators, and the new profession of sensitivity trainers. Being inclusive, we're told, is the way of equality.

EQUALITY AND INCLUSIVENESS seem to dominate discussions about the Boy Scouts these days. It would seem natural that a voluntary organization like the Boy Scouts should be as inclusive as possible to bring in members. Psychologists Roy Baumeister and Mark Leary observed that, "Human beings are fundamentally and pervasively motivated by a need to belong."[26] Perhaps that explains why the Boy Scouts have made such a tremendous effort to include boys from all races, classes, religions, and backgrounds.

But inclusiveness must be balanced with exclusiveness. If everybody can join an organization in a society as diverse as ours, there ceases to be anything unique about being a member. Every organization must decide on a set of membership standards and requirements that only certain people can attain.

Furthermore, in a divided culture as ours, the Boy Scouts must face, as they clearly have, the reality that it is necessary to exclude when excess inclusion would mean the compromising of core principles. In other words, when the Boy Scouts adhere to a different set of values than some who might wish to become members, the organization must commit to a certain degree of exclusiveness.

The First Amendment to the U.S. Constitution protects the right of free association, which goes for the Boy Scouts as well as Scouting for All, for the College Republicans as well as the College Democrats, for the Catholic Church as well as the Presbyterian Church or the Jewish synagogue. Columnist Lew Rockwell observed, "Excluding someone from a private association is not an act of hatred, any more than excluding someone from a dinner party implies you want him to starve. The freedom to associate includes the freedom not to associate, and no free society worthy of the name can compromise that principle."[27]

Melanie Kirkpatrick, writing for the *Wall Street Journal,* considered that if every organization and group were bound to inclusiveness, true diversity and meaningfulness within civic culture would be erased. "Will homosexuals want religious fundamentalists infiltrating their organizations and attempting to 'save their souls'?" she asked. "Will the Ku Klux Klan enjoy lighting candles for Kwanzaa to appease their black members? Put simply, people should be free to associate with whomever they care to so long as the association is voluntary and peaceful. The Boy Scouts is a private group and has every right to include and exclude as it sees fit."[28]

The Boy Scouts do not organize as a militant hate group against homosexuals and atheists. In a 2000 position statement, the BSA said, "The BSA respects the rights of people and groups who hold values that differ from those encompassed in the Scout Oath and Law, and the BSA makes no effort to deny the rights of those whose views differ to hold their attitudes or opinions."[29] But it is the position of the Boy Scouts that those who do hold and profess different values from those in the Scout oath and law are, plain and simple, unable and unwilling to abide by the Scout oath and law.

Scouting is not for all. Scouting is for any boy who's willing to swear to uphold a code of conduct, on the basis of his sacred honor.

IT IS NOT too difficult to imagine an oath modeled after the Scout oath that would symbolize the values of a generation that has forgotten honor.

> On my self-esteem,
> I will do whatever feels good
> For myself:
> And to question authority,
> To help myself at all times,
> To keep myself physically gratified,
> Mentally interested,
> And morally tolerant.

Clearly, honor is no longer a mere point of confusion as Tocqueville described it. In the larger culture, honor is a dying moral commodity. University of Michigan legal scholar William Ian Miller wrote, "Honor . . . has hidden its face, moved to the back regions of consciousness, been kicked out of most public discourse regarding individuals; it can no longer be offered as a justification for action in many settings where once it would have constituted the only legitimate motive."[30]

There is an unavoidable link between the decline of traditional community and family institutions and the demise of honor. Individualism has made its radical advance. Newly liberated individuals have cast off their bonds to the institutions that once compelled them to find a place in service to others. Individuals no longer feel obligated to serve their neighbors, their fellow countrymen, their posterity, or their Creator.

In that environment, far from the days of Seton, Beard, and Baden-Powell, it is increasingly difficult for the Boy Scouts to function as openly as they once did in relationship to society. If the cultural elite continues to accept nothing other than all-inclusive moral relativism, the Boy Scouts will become altogether alienated from the rest of culture. Each time it is likened to the Taliban or even to the Religious Right, the Boy Scouts are projected further and further from the mainstream. According to Gertrude Himmelfarb, "Individuals, families, churches, and communities cannot operate in isolation, cannot long maintain values at odds with those legitimized by the state and popularized by culture. It takes a great effort of will and intellect for the individual to decide for himself that something is immoral and to act on that belief when the law declares it legal and the culture deems it acceptable."[31] For that reason alone, there is good reason to be concerned about the marginalization of the Boy Scouts.

Given the state of American culture, one is naturally led to wonder if there's any hope for honor. William J. Bennett, former secretary of education and author of *The Book of Virtues*, addressed the U.S. Naval Academy in 1997 with the question, "Does honor have a future?" Bennett began with a warning: "If we do not confront the soft relativism that is currently disguised as a virtue, we will find ourselves morally and intellectually disarmed." Honor is being diminished, he observed, because "America has become a jaded society that no longer has a taste for simple things and that tends to equate freedom with license."

Bennett concluded that honor has a bright future if we "dedicate ourselves to principles of freedom that imply as much responsibility and discipline as they do independence and choice."[32]

"Let us pursue and teach the simple things," he said. If Bennett is correct in his diagnosis of honor's demise and his prescription for America's renewal of honor, society would do well to turn to one of the few institutions remaining that continues to pursue and teach the simple things.

If honor is to have a future, the Boy Scouts of America must take the lead.

CHAPTER 4

★★★

The Flight
from Manhood

Time to get up," said my uncle Ernie through the soaked red fabric of my three-man Northwest Territory dome tent, his voice barely audible against the rush of the Quinault River below our camp and the rain descending steadily from the canopy of the Olympics rain forest. The first clap of thunder had hit just after Brad, Tristan, and I had finished our dinner of canned ravioli the previous evening, and the biggest raindrops I'd ever seen followed within seconds of the thunder. We rushed to cover our backpacks with tarps and garbage bags and headed for cover in the tent.

Through the night, it seemed every drop of moisture in the heavens was making collective descent on Olympic National Park. In such circumstances, one takes to heart the phrase "Be prepared." I had forgotten to bring a rain fly for my tent, but Tristan had brought a big blue tarp.

But by morning, my tent and Tristan's tarp were insufficient shelter. It was only the second day of a seven-day journey across the mountains and forests of the Olympic Mountains, and even my waterproof sleeping bag had failed, a fact I realized long before it was time to get up. It had been an uncomfortable night. Fortunately, the rain stopped by the time we stepped out of the tent.

Within an hour, we were ready for action; oatmeal and granola bars were consumed, rain-laden sleeping bags were rolled and strapped to backpacks, and Ernie delivered a speech about his expectations of the day's adventures. Ernie was an assistant Scoutmaster in the tradition of his father, Ed, who was also along for the Olympics trek. Ernie organized most of the fifty-mile hikes, along with numerous shorter hikes and climbing expeditions, during my time in Troop 174.

Not long after leaving camp, we came to the crossing of the rumbling Quinault. The river was shoulder-deep, one hundred feet wide, bitter cold, and raging like white water so that the bridge had long ago been washed away. In its current state, even Cameron called it a dangerous crossing.

Cameron, an ex-Marine, county sheriff's deputy, and assistant Scoutmaster, rigged up the loose rope tied around trees on opposite banks for the purpose of transporting packs across the river. He began by tightening the rope on one end, and then he crossed over a narrow, slanting, fallen tree to the other side where he conducted the same routine of knots and tightenings. Then he shouted, "*Vaminos!*" (Spanish for "let's go"), and Ben settled a pair of carabiners on the rope by which he attached his own pack. One by one, with the strains of manipulating the rope and carabiners, the packs crossed the Quinault River. Cameron had engineered a first-class pulley system, and within an hour, all twelve packs were safely—and dryly—across the river.

Then it was time for us to cross the treacherous log to get to the other side. The tree ranged in elevation above the water from three feet on one end to perhaps seven feet on the other, but it was the only means for crossing. It was an intensive balancing act.

By the time this was accomplished, the sun had debuted through the clouds and it was time for lunch. Most of us pulled out our wet sleeping bags, unrolled them, and set them in the sun to dry a bit, watching misty vapors rise into the warming air. Knowing that the day ahead would be long and strenuous, Ernie urged us to hasten lunchtime and get back on the trail.

And so, we set out again just after noon. At first, the hiking wasn't much of a challenge. Then, the hills got steeper. Soon we were ascending higher and higher into the mountains, and then snow covered the ground. The debris from a massive avalanche—snow, sticks, and stones—blocked a significant portion of the trail at one point, and we had to crawl up and over it.

Eventually, the hiking smoothed out as we entered a sparsely wooded plain with majestic mountains flanking us on either side. But the trail was invisible beneath the snow. Ben and Cameron worked together with map and compass to discern the best route through the low divide. We stopped to rest and eat at a ranger station in the middle of the snowy plains.

After a few hours maneuvering through the snow-covered plains, we descended into a glacial valley where the trail became visible again. A subalpine lake, flowing from the August melt of a small glacier, graced the landscape. We decided on a refreshing swim—not as cold as one might expect—and some of the guys mounted a small cliff above the lake and dove in.

Without drying off, we quickly resumed the hike. The descent became steeper, the path more treacherous. Giant fallen, old-growth trees lay along an extensive stretch of the trail, and at one point it seemed we were competitors in a real Olympic hurdling contest. Sometimes it was over the tree, other times under. Either way was a problem for a backpack; the straps and buckles snagged on tree branches.

This continued until the middle of the evening when we finally arrived at the tree across the Hayes River that led to our campground, twelve adventurous miles from where we had started the day. We crossed the tree, ate a late dinner, put up the tents, hung our food in bear bags, and headed into our damp sleeping bags for the night.

Of such experiences, men are made.

YET THERE ARE those who would say that a week in the wilderness with cougars, bears, and mosquitoes is a worthless task. We don't need strong, manly men tried by the paths of the outdoors, hardened by the trails of adventure, enlivened by the experience of fellowship with like-minded youths, dedicated to God, America, and family. Instead, we need a man who "rejects the performance principles governing the established societies; a type of man who has rid himself of the aggressiveness and brutality that are inherent in the organization of established society and their hypocritical, puritan morality; a type of man who is biologically incapable of fighting wars and creating suffering; a type of man who has a good conscience of joy and pleasure, and who works collectively and individually for a social and natural environment in which such an existence becomes possible."[1] Those are the words of leftist philosopher Herbert Marcuse in a 1967 address to the Congress of the Dialectics of Liberation in London.

In 1910, another kind of man was wanted, not a fantastical new man for a utopian world. John L. Alexander wrote in the opening chapter of the Boy Scout handbook, "The Boy Scout of today must be chivalrous, manly, and gentlemanly. He should be unselfish. He should show courage. He must do his duty. He must show benevolence and thrift. He should be loyal to his country."[2]

Needless to say, there are two definitions of manhood that seem fixed in a bloody fight to the death on the stage of modern culture.

The Boy Scouts are holding for the traditional view of manhood. That isn't to say that the Boy Scouts are, as their critics suggest, dwellers in a secluded colony where a lingering haze of naivety keeps them oblivious to world changes. Daniel Carter Beard wrote in *Scouting* magazine nine decades ago: "The wilderness is gone, the buckskin man is gone, the painted Indian has hit the trail over the Great Divide, the hardships and privations of pioneer life which did so much to develop sterling manhood are now but a legend in history, and we must depend upon the Boy Scout movement to produce the MEN of the future."[3]

To the founders of Scouting, the men of the future were the men of the past insofar as their manliness was concerned. For the never-changing nature of men is, according to Camille Paglia, "aggressive, unstable, combustible. It is the most creative cultural force in history."[4] Christina Hoff Sommers, author of *The War on Boys,* wrote, "Traditional male traits such as aggression, competitiveness, risk-taking, and stoicism—constrained by virtues of valor, honor, and self-sacrifice—are essential to the well-being and safety of our society."[5] In its Greek origins, the word "manliness" was *andreia,* meaning "courage." In Latin, *virtus* was the word for manliness, a word from which we get "virtue." In any case, as Lord Robert Baden-Powell settled, "God made men to be *men.*"[6]

Times have changed, the founders of Scouting recognized, but still there is a need for young men to grow up, to study for and enter manhood, to fight and to conquer, to experience the wilderness. Young men need to know creation in its reality, not fabricated by pop culture or the temporary technologies of instant gratification but felt in the innermost spiritual longings of the male nature. It's why Troop 174 crossed the Olympic Mountains through snowfields and rain forests, why we spent other summers in the Cascade Mountains as guests of the marmot and the black bear, taming the wind-swept lookouts and ancient glaciers on the Northern Loop trail of Mount Rainier National Park, exploring the less traveled parts of Yellowstone, mastering the rugged hills and flat buffalo plains of Philmont Scout Ranch in New Mexico, conquering the deadly, jagged rocks of the Grand Tetons.

There were times in my Scouting experience I wanted to be home in my nice, warm bed, but survival afforded me no such option. There were times I wanted to stay in my sleeping bag in the early morning hours, but the challenge of experiencing God's creation suggested a different course. One learns resolve, preparedness, and duty in the outdoors.

Every spring, Troop 174 ventures to the snowfields above Mount Rainier's Paradise Base Camp to construct snow caves and igloos. We spend the night in the side of the mountain where preparedness is the only option.

In May, the troop goes to Ocean Shores State Park along the Pacific. Days and nights are spent in the rolling dunes and beach streams competing in vigorous games of capture the flag and kick the can. And in the afternoons, we play the ultimate ocean camp game on the beach: P-ball. P-ball is no-rules football, dirt and sweat, a kind of warfare that separates the men from the boys.

THAT'S HARDLY how modern culture sends its boys to become men. "We don't know how to initiate boys into men and . . . we're not sure we really want to. We want to socialize them, to be sure, but away from all that is fierce, and wild, and passionate," wrote John Eldredge, author of the best-selling *Wild at Heart*.[7] Social institutions have devalued the importance of "fierce, wild, and passionate" male activities that develop character while channeling aggression. According to Christina Hoff Sommers, "In a great number of American schools, gender reformers have succeeded in expunging many activities that young boys enjoy: dodge ball, cops and robbers, reading or listening to stories about battles and war heroes."[8] "Experts" have innovated new alternative activities for boys in school. For fear that childish male aggression on the playground may lead to school shootings, feminist-trained educators steer boys toward alternatives like quilting and scoreless games, and classic classroom stories of heroism and valor are replaced by soft Mr. Rogers-like tales.

A few years ago the Seattle public schools required hundreds of middle school students to participate in a costly "Challenge Day" that featured sensitivity seminars; crying was encouraged and self-esteem was preached. Naturally, boys rejected the ordeal. One boy called the seminars a "psycho cry-fest."[9] Psycho cry-fests are the latest in the theoretical art of socialization whereby the almighty experts seek to socially engineer Herbert Marcuse's sissified man.

Yet the real task at hand is not socialization but civilization. We have forgotten that. We have ignored the history of civilizations—West and East—built on the sweat and blood of succeeding generations of men who understood the importance of honor, valor, self-sacrifice, and virtue. Humankind survives with a sense of responsibility for writer Russell Kirk's "permanent things," which transcend the flesh and concern the things of the spirit. Manhood is a matter of serious spiritual responsibilities; culture must work together, with fathers in the lead, to civilize young men. Christina Hoff Sommers noted, "All societies confront the problem of civilizing their children, particularly the male ones. History teaches that masculinity constrained by morality is powerful and constructive; it also teaches that masculinity without ethics is dangerous and destructive."[10]

Indeed, boys are more aggressive than girls, so it is necessary for society to channel that aggression in culturally edifying directions. It is imperative that boys experience male and female influence in the formative stages of life and character. On one hand, women are the civilizing factor in society. Boys need mothers to nurture and feed them both physically and spiritually, to teach social norms, to enforce respect, to demand manners. On the other hand, boys need fathers to set an example as role models, to teach male responsibility, to discipline, and to challenge. Fathers are missing from too many homes in America.

Without stable families, churches, and involvement in the Boy Scouts, the civilization of young men is largely a failed endeavor in contemporary society. Observed Dr. Michael Gurian, author of *A Fine Young Man,* "Our culture's economic stresses, family breakdowns, and forgetfulness of the developmental needs of adolescent males have made it one of the only cultures on human record that gives adolescent males so little intimate nurturing by elder males."[11] Today, the family and society are failing because men fail to be real fathers to their sons, and society has increasingly discouraged outlets for male aggression and inlets for character development. Divorce divides too many families. Churches fail to speak for manly virtue.

The concept of initiation, once central to manhood, has been forgotten in the modern mind. "Most men have never been initiated into manhood," wrote John Eldredge. "They have never had anyone show them how to do it, and especially how to fight for their heart. The failure of so many fathers, the emasculating culture, and the passive church have left men without direction."[12]

Young males are being left behind in contemporary culture. "The boy's hardwired drive to engage in masculine nurturing systems is hardly supplied software in our culture," wrote Gurian. "These days, the lack of time and responsibility that adult

and fathering males have and take, and the plethora of social attacks on male nurturing systems have combined to injure male
adolescent development."[13] As influential as the Boy Scouts, military service, athletic competition, and other forms of masculine
development have become, those venues have found themselves
contending with a broader culture that disdains traditional
manly virtues.

HOW DID THE American male become unmanly? The answer is
twofold.

First, manly virtue, the product of honor, has gone by the
wayside. Christian churches are largely to blame for this problem.
Virtue need not be weak; but contemporary Christianity, steeped
in seeker-sensitive worship and gutless ecumenism, has made it
weaker than ever before. Even those who speak of virtue are guilty
of emaciating it.

Modern man cares little for passionate virtue, and the contemporary doctrines of moral relativism complement his tastes quite
well. The media frequently displays a passive man sitting before a
television set in his recliner, watching football with a Budweiser in
his right hand and a remote control in his left. Or there is the active
man of media: the wrestler cursing and swearing at his opponent as
he pummels him, and Justin Timberlake ripping off Janet Jackson's
breast cover at the 2004 Super Bowl. A large and growing breed of
man reads *Playboy* and *Hustler,* views porn videos, promiscuously
pursues gratuitous sex, and exploits women in general.

It was actually the first problem, the emasculation of virtue
that gave rise to the second problem: the feminization of America.
What has been called women's liberation was actually the consequence of the moral liberation of men. Beginning in the 1950s and
becoming a full reality by the 1960s, restraints on male behavior
were lifted, responsibility shifted, and honor forgotten altogether.
While so many brave young men fought in Vietnam, another distinguished group of young men stayed behind to dodge the draft
and protest the war on their campuses while impregnating girls
and taking drugs.

The irresponsibility of an entire generation of males gave reason to their female counterparts to seek dramatic change. Men had been irresponsible with their power. Respect and understanding between the sexes was diminished greatly. For women, the answer was to seek full equality in society by wresting authority from the hands of dishonorable men. Feminists were not offended by manliness itself; they were driven to action by the perversions of manliness and the incompatibilities of those perversions with women. Women sought to escape the divided home, to fill the gaps left by men of questionable character.

Under normal circumstances, men should have been called to account long ago for their sins. But the same breakdown in the family that gave rise to the prevailing youth culture caused a confusion of gender roles. The counterpart to man was driven from his side when the spirit of individualism and egalitarianism called her. Women should have scolded a generation of men for neglecting virtue, but the traditional relationship between males and females, unequal as it may have been, was entirely cast aside.

While society has ignored the distinctions between men and women in the pursuit of equality for women, manly nature remains as beastly and in need of restraint as ever before, a fact that has been far from beneficial for women. Instead of popular culture following the demands of the *traditional* feminist movement to cease its grotesque exploitations of women and sex, the popular culture has exploited women and sex even more. Neither masculinity nor femininity has triumphed, but the egalitarian opponents of the traditional family have. And equality, more appropriately labeled "sameness," has failed to equalize the sexes, but it has succeeded in confusing them.

And boys are the most confused. Appropriate male behavior is no longer defined by the culture; fathers are missing; young men are trapped in the mass-marketed world of popular culture; the outdoors and the conquering spirit are relegated to history books that aren't taught in the public schools. The choice for honor is hidden from view, somewhere behind the rubble of an ailing civilization.

AND INDEED, our very civilization is at stake. Half a century ago, C. S. Lewis witnessed the growing demise of honorable manhood. "We make men without chests and expect of them virtue and enterprise," he commented. "We laugh at honour and are shocked to find traitors in our midst. We castrate and bid the geldings be fruitful."[14] It is nothing less than a contrast between survival and extinction, freedom and slavery, honor and treason.

Honor is the missing ingredient in our contemporary concept of masculinity. It isn't that society has completely abnegated the task of raising men from boyhood, but it has approached the gargantuan endeavor in a radically new and different way than did our forefathers in millennia of Western tradition. This new approach to raising boys into men is nearly ignorant of honor altogether.

Instead of growing into responsible, honorable men, modern males become one of two polar extremes. "One extreme," wrote Terrence Moore, "suffers from an excess of manliness, or from misdirected and unrefined manly energies. The other suffers from a lack of manliness, a total want of manly spirit. Call them barbarians and wimps."[15] Culture works with amazing efficiency to encourage and cultivate the two extremes at the same time.

There is hardly a middle ground. On one hand, boys are told to be more sensitive and emotion-driven, like women. Of course, men and women are very different on emotional and physical levels. According to James Q. Wilson: "Men are more aggressive than women. Though child-rearing practices may intensify or moderate this difference, the difference will persist and almost surely rests on biological factors. In every known society, men are more likely than women to play roughly, drive recklessly, fight physically, and assault ruthlessly, and these differences appear early in life. . . . As they grow up, men are more likely than women to cause trouble in school, to be alcoholics or drug addicts, and to commit crimes."[16]

Indeed, libraries of data in the fields of psychology, neuroscience, and endocrinology illustrate the natural existence of masculinity in the male mind and body. Certainly, there are variations in the specific traits of individuals, but, by and large, males are better than females at spatial reasoning, risk taking, competition, and emotional control.[17] Women, by contrast, are more nurturing, verbally inclined, and peaceful. No matter how the issue of gender is viewed, men cannot become women.

But the wimps would have us forget the distinctions between male and female. In his treatise challenging the Boy Scouts' views of masculinity, Dr. Jay Mechling contended, "A boy who emerges from the Boy Scouts with a rigid, traditional view of masculinity, in short, will not have had the role models appropriate for the twenty-first century." Instead, Mechling saw the Scout of the future as a sensitized, relativistic young man, numbed to his potential perceptions of biases about women and homosexuals. "With proper attention to defining masculinity positively, misogyny and homophobia would wither away eventually, first in the public culture of the Boy Scout troop and then in the private folk culture of the adolescent boys themselves."[18] Mechling's views—disguised by the buzzwords "misogyny" and "homophobia"—that boys and men need not distinguish between homosexual and heterosexual and male and female are precisely the confusion resulting from moral relativism and radical egalitarianism.

The causes that give rise to barbarians in modern society are the same as the causes of the wimps. Society has forgotten character, honor, and manliness, and the resulting problem is far worse than the boy problem of a century ago. We felt the wave of school shootings by boys that paralyzed American schools during the late 1990s. It is no wonder that boys find alternatives for releasing their pressure by becoming involved in gangs, drugs, and violence.

The past few generations of American men have been intellectual products of the sanitized, psychologized public school classroom; moral products of the youth culture; spiritual products of self-worship. We drift toward the new man of Herbert Marcuse, though in practice the new man is a wimp and a barbarian and not a god, and away from the ancient heir of Scouting spoken of by John Alexander in the first Boy Scout handbook.

MASCULINITY IS in trouble. In this present crisis, how are we as a society to go about the task of civilizing young men? The answer to the question should not be difficult; academic scholars need not theorize on the issue, for the answer already exists in the vast experience of history and human nature.

First, boys need structured activities consistent with the demands of the unchanging male nature. According to Sommers, boys need defined restraints and order, but they do not need to be feminized. "Efforts to civilize boys with honor codes, character education, manners, and rules of good sportsmanship are necessary and effective, and fully consistent with their masculine natures. Efforts to feminize them with dolls, quilts, noncompetitive games, girl-centered books, and feelings exercises will fail; though they will succeed in making millions of boys quite unhappy."[19]

Second, boys need heroes. "I am perfectly certain," Baden-Powell wrote, "that bravery and self-sacrifice, the principle among manly virtues, can be developed in boys, and one of the best means to this end is to present to them concrete examples not of dead and gone heroes, but rather of present-day men in the street, or boys of their own kind who have done great deeds."[20] Baden-Powell believed that the world is full of heroes and wise men who must be brought to the service of the following generations. Boys, he believed, need role models to set an example, teach prudence, and inspire valor. That means men must make a conscious effort to be heroes to boys by being available as fathers, grandfathers, Scoutmasters, neighbors, and pastors. "Masculinity is bestowed by masculinity," wrote John Eldredge.[21]

Third, boys must be actively challenged to become heroes themselves. Terrence Moore explained: "First, a clear challenge must be issued to young males urging them to become the men their grandfathers and great-grandfathers were. This challenge must be clear, uncompromising, engaging, somewhat humorous, and inspiring. It cannot seem like a tired, fusty, chicken-little lament on the part of the old and boring, but must be seen as the truly revolutionary and cutting edge effort to recover authentic manliness. Second, a new generation of scholars must tell the tale of how men used to become men and act manfully, and how we as a nation have lost our sense of true manliness."[22]

Finally, boys must be fully initiated into manhood. "Initiation," explained John Eldredge, "doesn't take place at a school desk; it takes place in the field, where simple lessons about land and animals and seasons turn into larger lessons about life and self and God. Through each test comes a revelation."[23] Sounds like a task for the Boy Scouts, through which men and boys get together in the outdoors to learn about life.

What organization is better equipped to help resolve the crisis in masculinity than the Boy Scouts of America? Who more ably articulates the meaning of manly honor in our time than the Scouts? As one of the world's greatest experts on boys and character development, Baden-Powell declared, "Everything on two legs that calls itself a boy has God in him. Although he may—through the artificial environment of modern civilization—be the most arrant little thief, liar, and filth-monger unhung." Baden-Powell was not deterred by the monstrous task of turning a bad boy into a good man. "Our job is to give him a chance," he asserted.[24]

Boy Scouting gave boys a chance because it satisfied two of their needs. In a 1914 article for *Good Housekeeping*, Thornton W. Burgess wrote, "As a member of a Boy Scout patrol, under the right kind of a Scoutmaster," a boy has "two natural cravings of boy nature gratified"—the desire to "belong to a gang" and to "worship a hero."[25] The Boy Scouts provided supervised activities that developed character, supplemented the work of the family, projected examples of adult role models, challenged, and initiated.

Of course, the reality is an entire cultural network of organizations is required to give boys a chance—including the family and the church. But the Boy Scouts are one of the few groups remaining on the American landscape doing its part, that understands and works to cultivate wholesome, positive masculinity. Author Michael Rosenthal has called Scouting a "cult of masculinity."[26]

Scouting is no cult, but its influence on masculinity is not to be underestimated. In the midst of the turmoil of culture, age, divided families, and a lack of spirituality, Scouting, observed James West, "takes the boy when he is beset with the new and bewildering experiences of adolescence and diverts his thoughts therefrom to wholesome and worthwhile activities."[27] Wholesome, that is, until homosexuals began invading the Boy Scouts of America.

CHAPTER 5

★★★

Morally Straight

In some parts of America these days, one can hardly mention the Boy Scouts without provoking contention about the Scouts' controversial policy restricting homosexuals from membership and leadership. Eighteen-year-old Matt Hill of Winston-Salem, North Carolina, came out as a homosexual at the age of fourteen and was forced out of his Scout troop. Hill founded a student organization at R. J. Reynolds High School called Students Promoting Equality Awareness and Knowledge to give voice to discrimination such as that practiced by the Boy Scouts.

In a debate with Hill on a North Carolina radio station, I pointed out that while it was true the Scouts had discriminated against him, his lifestyle was in direct contradiction to the Boy Scout oath. Thus, it was Matt Hill himself who had chosen to discriminate against the principles of Scouting by expressly choosing not to be "morally straight."

Hill said that to be morally straight means to accept people regardless of who they are and what choices they make.

"That's fine," I rebutted, "but the Boy Scouts don't have to accept all choices that people make. The Boy Scouts have defined morally straight to mean a certain type of character, and only the Boy Scouts of America can define what that type of character is. Morally straight means many things, and it includes a regard for the traditional, heterosexual marriage relationship."[1]

The Scout oath always has meant that, as I will demonstrate in this chapter, but Matt Hill and his allies in the homosexual movement would like to think that morally straight is flexible enough to conform to an alternative code of morals that are relative, that are personalized, that differ from person to person and place to place, that in the end aren't even morals at all.

Matt Hill is the latest in a twenty-five-year lineup of homosexual former Scouts and Scoutmasters who have brought attention to the Boy Scouts' exclusion of homosexuals. It all began in 1980 when seventeen-year-old Timothy Curran of Oakland, California, made a few headlines in the local Bay Area newspapers by choosing to date a male at Skyline High School's senior prom. At the time, Curran was a Boy Scout in Troop 37 of Berkeley with an outstanding application to become a Scoutmaster on his eighteenth birthday.[2]

The public announcement of Curran's homosexuality became an issue for executives in the East Bay Mount Diablo Boy Scout Council when it came time to consider Curran's Scoutmaster application. Timothy Curran was given the opportunity to appear before the executive council board at its office in Walnut Creek, California. After Curran affirmed his blatant rejection of Scout policies regarding moral behavior, the council told Curran he could not become a Scoutmaster. Chief Executive Officer Quentin Alexander stated, "Homosexuality and Boy Scouting are not compatible."[3]

Curran, along with the American Civil Liberties Union and the National Gay Task Force, filed a $520,000 lawsuit seeking an injunction against the Mount Diablo Council. The lawsuit claimed that the council had violated the California Civil Rights Act by its denial of "equal public accommodations."[4] BSA spokesman Lee Sneath said, "It was clearly understood that homosexuality was an immoral behavior and had no place in Scouting for youth or leaders. As an organization that stresses the values of the family, we believe that homosexuals do not provide the proper role model for youth membership."[5]

While Curran's lawsuit went from court to court over a period of seventeen years, Curran became an icon for the homosexual movement. He made appearances on television news programs and talk shows, portraying the Boy Scouts as a bigoted, homophobic organization. "I believe that the Boy Scouts demonstrated to me that they didn't have the faintest idea what scouting principles were all about," Curran told the *San Francisco Examiner,* as if Scouting should suddenly accept and teach homosexual behavior.[6]

One judge who heard Curran's case in 1990, Los Angeles Superior Court Judge Sally Disco, ruled that "the Boy Scouts were a business and thus subject to state civil rights law, which bars discrimination on the basis of sexual orientation, race, or religion."[7] Yet Disco recognized that the First Amendment right to free association trumped the California antidiscrimination code.

Curran and the ACLU appealed the Superior Court decision to the California Supreme Court, which it finally took up in 1998. The court ruled, along with their ruling on the Randall case (see chap. 11) that Judge Disco had made the correct decision eight years earlier.[8]

THE NATIONAL Boy Scouts didn't actually have an established membership code about homosexuality before 1978, a fact that has been used by critics to suggest the Boy Scouts have turned from an accepting, tolerant organization to something like the Ku Klux Klan. But by the same token, America didn't need a constitutional amendment banning homosexual "marriage" until 2004. Quite simply, society once found homosexuality to be such an egregious violation of moral norms that written policies were not even necessary in the U.S. Constitution or the BSA bylaws.

Like most of America, the Boy Scouts have always opposed homosexual behavior, a fact explored in the next chapter. The Boy Scouts, like society at large, began to discuss the topic of homosexuality in its publications only in the 1960s. A 1968 pamphlet for the personal fitness merit badge by Dr. J. Roswell Gallagher, chief of the Adolescent's Unit at Boston's Children's Medical Center, contained this on homosexuality: "[Homosexuality describes] a fixed adult pattern of behavior in which an individual is sexually attracted only to members of his own sex. Many boys before they become interested in girls develop strong friendships with other boys. This is perfectly normal and will lead to many strong friendships for the rest of their lives. It does not mean that they are homosexuals or are not manly or will not develop an interest in girls. As they grow up and widen their circle of friends and activities, they will become attracted to the opposite sex."[9]

An early 1970s Scoutmaster handbook warned of "the practices of a confirmed homosexual" boy who came to Scouting as a way to satisfy sexual appetites and "may be using his Scouting association to make contacts."[10] This warning was not unsubstantiated, and the rise of the homosexual movement forced the BSA to come up with its official policy banning homosexuals from membership and leadership in 1978. That policy was reiterated several times since. A statement in 1991 explained the official interpretation of controversial phrases in the Scout oath and law: "We believe that homosexual conduct is inconsistent with the requirement in the Scout Oath that a Scout be morally straight and in the Scout Law that a Scout be clean in word and deed and that homosexuals do not provide a desirable role model for Scouts."[11] And in 2002, the Scouts formed committees to consider the BSA's position on homosexuality, concluding that "homosexual conduct is inconsistent with the traditional values espoused in the Scout Oath and Law and that an avowed homosexual cannot serve as a role model for the values of the Oath and Law."[12]

Despite the hard-line policy on homosexuality, the Boy Scouts of America have mostly ignored several renegade local councils (see chap. 1) whose defiant policies and nondiscrimination codes range from "don't ask, don't tell" in Boston's Minuteman Council to the radical stance of the San Francisco Piedmont Council to accept openly homosexual leaders. The Scouts have successfully resisted smaller rebellions, such as a joint effort by several Illinois Cub Scout packs to accept homosexual Scoutmasters that ended in the disbanding of the packs.[13]

Some critics have alleged that the Boy Scouts stage a witch-hunt to root out homosexuals in the organization while caring little about heterosexual promiscuity and deviance. But the Boy Scouts of America isn't concerned only about homosexuality. It also teaches that sex outside marriage is wrong. The Boy Scout handbook is clear: "Sex should take place only between people who are married to each other. . . . An understanding of wholesome sexual behavior can bring lifelong happiness. Irresponsibility or ignorance, however, can cause a lifetime of regret. . . . Learn what is right."[14]

EVERY ENDURING society of the past has kept homosexuality, if not outlawed, stigmatized. Political scientist Harry V. Jaffa wrote:

> From ancient—and biblical—times, this practice has
> been regarded by the greatest legislators and moralists as
> a vicious sexual perversion. It is condemned equally by
> the Old and New Testaments, and by Plato in his Laws.
> Thomas Jefferson, in a criminal code written during
> the American Revolution, made it a felony in the same
> class as rape. In this he only followed the common law.
> Nor is the connection between this idea and the family
> unprecedented or unreasonable: Mankind as a whole is
> recognized by its generations, like a river which is one
> and the same while the ever-renewed cycles of birth and
> death flow on. But the generations are constituted—and
> can only be constituted—by the acts of generation
> arising from the conjunction of male and female. . . .
> Equally with rape and incest, homosexuality strikes at
> the authority and dignity of the family. The distinction
> between a man and a woman is as fundamental as any in
> nature, because it is the very distinction by which nature
> itself is constituted.[15]

All thirteen original states considered sodomy a criminal or common law offense, and it remained a punishable crime in all fifty states until 1961.[16] More than a dozen states continued to ban sodomy until 2003, when the U.S. Supreme Court ruled those laws unconstitutional.

Homosexuality is what medical doctors and psychologists historically have called a disorder. As a disorder, writes Christopher Wolfe, it is "an affliction for those who suffer from it."[17] Thus, when it comes to individual homosexuals, the issue must be dealt with sensitively.

But as a movement, homosexuality preaches an end to the traditional family. One could reasonably follow the logic of the family's demise to mean that the community and the nation would face their final days.

A result of moral relativism, the homosexual movement has been welcomed to the stage of American life. The contention of radical individualism—that there are no constraints when it comes to sexual behavior, personal lifestyle, or moral choices, the "anything goes" mentality—has facilitated for America not only a dead-end for the old social stigma against homosexuality, but an entirely remodeled culture conformed to homosexuals' political and sexual desires.

There is without question a great deal of confusion in American culture today. In our divided culture, temptations, ideologies, fanaticisms, and perversions run in a million different ways. In the midst of moral confusion, according to Dr. Joseph Nicolosi, "we see animal confused with human, sacred confused with profane, adult confused with child, male confused with female, and life confused with death—all of these traditionally the most profound of distinctions and separations, are now under siege."[18]

The siege began after World War II when Dr. Alfred Kinsey, in his 1948 book *Sexual Behavior in the Human Male,* claimed that homosexuality was a valid orientation, and that many people around the nation were in fact gay and lesbian.[19] Following Kinsey's loan of credibility to homosexuality, homosexual behavior began a gradual move toward becoming an accepted social behavior.[20] In 1964, Kinsey's followers founded the Sex Information and Education Council of the United States (SIECUS) to promote the homosexual agenda in education, health care, and government.[21]

The women's liberation movement of the 1960s became a natural ally for homosexuals. As the institutions of marriage and the family began their decline, the public stage was opened for homosexuals to proclaim a bold alternative to the traditional family.

In 1972, many of the eight hundred homosexual organizations then active in the United States met in Chicago for the convention of the National Coalition of Gay Organizations.[22] Convention delegates passed what they called the Gay Rights Platform, a series of proposals that at the time seemed nearly impossible:

- Amend all federal Civil Rights Acts, other legislation, and government controls to prohibit discrimination in employment, housing, public accommodations, and public services.
- Allow homosexuals in the military.
- Eliminate tax inequities.
- Eliminate barriers to homosexual immigrants.
- Require sex education in schools that is favorable to homosexuality.
- Provide federal funding for homosexual organizations.
- Enact similar policies in the states.[23]

Today, many of the platform planks are a reality, and the rest are not difficult to imagine being enacted in the near future.

On the scientific front, the American Psychological Association first used "normal" to describe homosexuality in 1975.[24] The National Institute for Mental Health declared that homosexuality ought to be promoted in schools as normal.[25]

But homosexuality has its toll in health. In the early 1980s, the AIDS virus was discovered. For several years, the vast majority of AIDS patients were gay men. As AIDS spread, taking many lives, homosexual activists took to the streets, rallying for federal health care dollars and public sympathy. Largely as a result of the sentiments aroused in the spread of AIDS, public opinion began to shift in favor of homosexual rights.

The homosexual movement has suddenly become the single greatest threat to the traditional family structure in America. The homosexual agenda is being integrated into society with great vigor and strategic precision. Many of America's civil rights laws have been amended to include "sexual orientation" and "gender identity" in the same list as race, sex, national origin, and so on. Educators in America's public schools pursue the acceptance of

homosexuality as a valid form of diversity. The media has ex-
alted sexual diversity and increasingly, homosexuality is becoming mainstream on television with reality television programs
like *Queer Eye for the Straight Guy*. Most damaging, "homosexual
marriage" has become a reality in San Francisco, New York, Seattle, Massachusetts, and New Mexico, and soon will become
legal in all of America if conservative Christian opposition is as
minimal as it has been on most other moral issues of the past
several decades.

What's so stunning about the dramatic success of the homosexual movement in a health-conscious, scientistic age is that homosexuality is far from being a healthy or even scientifically credible
behavior. To date, no researcher has been able to locate the so-called
gay gene. According to Dr. Joseph Nicolosi, the reason is "there is
no such thing as a gay person. Gay is an identity seized upon by an
individual to resolve painful emotional challenges."[26]

Dr. Joel Gelernter of Yale said of attempted genetic explana-
tions, "All were announced with great fanfare; all were greeted
without skepticism in the popular press; all are now in disre-
pute."[27] Despite the evidence to the contrary, it has become largely
accepted that sexual orientations other than heterosexuality exist.
Some homosexual organizations now identify up to two dozen different sexual orientations or gender identities. Instead of treating
homosexuality as an invalid perversion of sexuality, it is tolerated,
encouraged, and celebrated.

Even much of the medical community has become numbed
to the scientific incredibility of homosexuality. At the American
Medical Association Convention in May 2001, Dr. Alfred Cox of
the Rhode Island Medical Association proposed a resolution tar-
geting the Boy Scouts. The resolution said, in part: "It is the policy
of some national youth organizations to exclude homosexuals
solely because of their sexual orientation. . . . Sexual orientation
is not an appropriate reason for discrimination and exclusion. . . .
Homosexuality is a significant health issue due to its associated
risk for adolescent suicide. . . . Therefore, BE IT RESOLVED that
our American Medical Association ask all national youth oriented

organizations to reconsider any and all exclusionary policies that are based on sexual orientation as one step to lower the increased risk of suicide in the adolescent homosexual population."[28]

The AMA passed the resolution, essentially saying that the Boy Scouts' moral standards equate to teen suicide. Obviously, no such connection can be made within reason. Certainly, the resolution lacked warrants for its outrageous claims.

For many defenders of Scouting, it has become cliché to respond to the arguments advanced by groups like the AMA that regardless of what the Boy Scouts believe, they have a right to believe it. Such a defense works well in legal circumstances, but it is not the most important defense in practical, cultural matters. Just because something is a right doesn't mean it is good. Of course the Boy Scouts have a right to believe in the oath and law. But the most important thing about their belief in the oath and law is its basis in honor and in good, sound principle.

Scouting teaches its youth to be physically strong and morally straight, to be clean, and to respect others. Scouting also teaches young men valuable lifesaving skills that have resulted in the rescue of thousands since 1910, a record that the Boy Scouts should be commended for by a medical organization.

Dr. Dale O'Leary of *Heartbeat News* criticized the AMA's resolution. To accuse the BSA of causing suicide, she wrote, is to weaken the level of respect for the AMA among patients and citizens.[29] "The AMA appears to have accepted the unsubstantiated claim that the numerous psychological problems and self-destructive behavior found among persons who self-identify as gay, lesbian, or bisexual (GLB) are caused by social discrimination. It has ignored substantial evidence that these negative outcomes are related to the homosexuality itself."[30]

The reality is that homosexuality is a dangerous lifestyle, and health professionals should have the character to look beyond politics to real life. O'Leary cited a 1998 study that revealed the higher incidence of risky behaviors among homosexual teenagers. Homosexual youth are twice as likely to use alcohol, fourteen times as likely to use cocaine, and nearly twice as likely to be sexually active (81 percent). Nearly 6 percent of sexually active gays under age nineteen are positive for the HIV virus.[31]

The health liability alone is reason enough to keep homosexuality out of the Boy Scouts. After all, "a Scout is clean."

CHAPTER 6

★★★

Scoutmasters
Who Abuse

The larger issue is sexual abuse of children. In a youth organization with a broad age range as in the Boy Scouts, molestation is a real possibility, even with stringent policies in place to prevent it. There's no denying that homosexual abuse and molestation is a major liability for the Boy Scouts of America.

Critics of Scouting claim there is little risk of molestation by opening membership to homosexual leaders and boys. "The fear of molestation, it seems, is a weak reason for wanting to exclude openly homosexual teens and men from the Boy Scouts," wrote University of California–Davis professor Jay Mechling in his book about Scouting. "To exclude all avowed homosexuals because some might molest a boy is to approach the problem from the wrong direction and to punish thousands of gay teens and men, while at the same time making it highly unlikely that there will be fewer sexual predators among the members."[1] The facts contradict Mechling.

But Mechling also mischaracterized the position of the Boy Scouts. In fact, the Boy Scouts of America maintain there is no direct correlation between homosexuality and pedophilia. BSA spokesman Gregg Shields wrote to me, "Our Youth Protection policy and our policy on homosexuals as members are distinct. . . . It doesn't matter if an avowed homosexual claims to be celibate, or does not have a record as a pedophile; if you say that you are homosexual, you will not be in the Boy Scouts. These two policies are crystal clear, can stand on their own, and speak for themselves."[2]

In court cases involving homosexual Scoutmasters, the Boy Scouts have consistently maintained that homosexuals are excluded because they are improper role models for boys and fail to live up to the Scout oath and law. As Shields said, the official reasoning for exclusion of homosexuals can stand on its own. The premise of the official Boy Scouts of America position may be incomplete, but in the end, homosexuals are kept out of the organization just as effectively as if there had been recognition of a link between homosexual and pedophilic behavior.

But as I am under no burden to represent the official position of the Boy Scouts of America, we ought to consider the relationship between homosexuality and pedophilia. As Dr. Paul Cameron of the Family Research Institute pointed out in his book *Right or Wrong: Should the Boy Scouts Include Homosexuals?*, homosexuality is not a natural orientation but a behavior defined by the Centers for Disease Control and Prevention as "males who have sex with males."[3] By definition then, "all molestations of Boy Scouts by Scoutmasters are homosexual. There is no risk of heterosexual child molestation within the Boy Scouts."[4]

Even if someone describes himself as heterosexual, his homosexual behavior alone is enough to qualify him as a homosexual. Using that rationale, it would seem only natural to correlate homosexuality with the risk of molestation in the Scouts if it can be proven that homosexuals have a higher rate of pedophilia in the general population besides the male-only demographics of Scouting.

Consider these statistics. A 1992 report titled "The Proportions of Heterosexual and Homosexual Pedophiles among Sex Offenders against Children" in the *Journal of Sex and Marital Therapy* revealed that child molestation is proportionally eight times higher by homosexual perpetrators as heterosexual perpetrators.[5] A study for the Archives of Social Behavior in 2000 indicated that "the rate of homosexual attraction is 6-20 times higher among pedophiles."[6] When researchers in the same study asked convicted, imprisoned pedophilic sex offenders to identify their sexual attraction, "Eighty-six percent of offenders against males [boys] described themselves as homosexual or bisexual."[7] A 1985 *Psychological Reports* study showed that homosexual teachers are 90 to 100 percent more likely to engage in sexual behavior with students than heterosexual teachers; and on sheer numbers, homosexuals account for between 25 and 40 percent of all child molestation.[8] Heterosexuals outnumber homosexuals by more than twenty to one in the general population, but statistics consistently show that approximately one in three cases of child sex abuse are by homosexuals.[9]

Compared to the small percentage of homosexuals in the general population, homosexuals sexually molest children at a rate so high that Americans would be foolish to dismiss the issue for the sake of tolerance. As FBI child abuse expert Kenneth Lanning affirmed, "Nonincestuous homosexual male pedophiles" are "the most persistent and prolific child molesters known to the criminal justice system."[10]

Dr. Judith Reisman, a veteran antipornography crusader and author of *Kinsey: Crimes and Consequences*, argued that homosexuals are anxious to use young people for sexual gratification, not only because of the experience but also because of the vulnerability of young people to become homosexual themselves.[11] The system of homosexuality is self-perpetuating, which makes the movement itself so dangerous.

OF ALL YOUTH-ORIENTED groups in the United States, Reisman said "the Boy Scouts provide the most ideal situation" for men to molest young boys.[12] Patrick Boyle, author of the 1994 book *Scout's Honor: Sexual Abuse in America's Most Trusted Institution*, observed that Scouting "brings young males together just as their sexual curiosity is awakening, and provides older males to guide them to manhood."[13] Sometimes, these older males find the perfect conditions in Scouting for molesting boys and adolescents. According to Lanning, "There are certain elements in Scouting that make it high risk" for child molestation.[14] Another expert, Dr. Eugene Abel, contended that though Scouting leader is not the only position attractive to sex offenders, "it is an ideal one for the pedophile because the Scout leader is boss."[15]

Responding to isolated incidents of homosexual behavior and molestation as early as 1911, the Boy Scouts headquarters kept an ongoing red-flag list of men who were inappropriate role models for boys. This file included men with a record of problematic alcoholism, criminal convictions, and extortion of troop coffers. Each folder included detailed information about the man and why he had been kicked out of the program or rejected for leadership. James West boasted about the effectiveness of the list: "No other organization has it. No other organization has the conception of its value, because no other organization to my knowledge has availed itself of its use."[16]

By the late 1930s, the Boy Scouts of America were desperate to find adult volunteers to work with the growing masses of boys who had enrolled. Thus, Scouting executives and troop leaders who made choices about volunteers were often, in the words of a 1930s BSA internal memo, "careless and casual."[17] BSA national headquarters began to set more stringent guidelines for leadership in the spirit of the Boy Scouts' bylaws: "No person shall be approved as a leader unless, in the judgment of the corporation, that person possesses the moral, educational, and emotional qualities deemed necessary for leadership."[18]

Because of the image problems that could arise from admitting a problem with homosexual molestation, the Boy Scouts were quiet—almost ignorant—on the issue for decades. But coinciding with the rise of homosexuality in the 1970s came a dramatic increase in sex abuse in the Boy Scouts.

Before the Boy Scouts realized they had a developing problem, the North American Man-Boy Love Association actively encouraged its members to join the Boy Scouts and the Big Brothers, and pictures of uniformed Scouts appeared frequently in NAMBLA newsletters.[19] Alfred Kinsey's SIECUS gave academic credibility to NAMBLA's sick activism by publishing "The SIECUS Guide to Child/Adult Sex" in 1970.[20]

NAMBLA and SIECUS maintained an impressive corps of die-hard pederasts in Boy Scout troops around the country. In Oregon, Scoutmaster Franklin Mathias was convicted for trying or performing more than 1,100 sex acts with boys over a period of thirty years.[21] In 1974, a group of homosexual men founded a Scout troop at a Presbyterian church in an impoverished section of New Orleans with the intention of turning it into a child-sex ring, and they did just that while building a national reputation in the underground pedophile community. The homosexual Scoutmasters took advantage of the poverty of their Scouts (only four of eighteen troop members lived with their fathers) and were involved in exchanging pornographic pictures, tales, and boys themselves with other child-sex operations. A photo developer alerted police to evidence of the vile troop, and the infamous "gay scout ring" ended in seventeen arrests.[22]

In the most of the past thirty years, "sex abuse has accounted for more than half of all leaders banned from the Boy Scouts."[23] Between 1971 and 1991, according to attorney Michael Rothschild who obtained a court order to review the confidential BSA files, 1,871 Scout leaders were banned from troops or rejected on application for sex abuse. That's an average of sixty-eight adults banned per year for molestation.[24]

A list of newspaper headlines compiled by Focus on the Family in 2001 reflects the overwhelming need to prevent young men from abuse in an organization as broad as the BSA:

- "Boy Scouts ignored warning about molester, Edmonton court hears" (Canadian Press, September 10, 2001)
- "Scout molestation case opening" (AP, July 8, 2001), regarding plea of innocence to 130 charges against Massachusetts Boy Scout leader
- "Scout leader faces boy sex rap" (New York Daily News, May 23, 2001)
- "Former scout leader guilty of sex charge" (Ottawa Citizen, May 23, 2001)

- "Scouts leader charged with sex crimes" (*Evansville Courier & Press*/AP, May 2, 2001)
- "Scout leader's sentence criticized" (*Pittsburgh Post-Gazette,* April 25, 2001) regarding assistant Scoutmaster sentenced for abusing three boys on an overnight campout
- "Former boy scout assistant charged with molesting scouts 15 years ago" (*Ohio News,* April 13, 2001)
- "Former Scout administrator sentenced for molesting boys" (AP, February 22, 2001)
- "Former Scout leader arrested" (Newsday.com, January 22, 2001), regarding twenty misdemeanor counts
- "Ex-scout leader charged in molestation" (*Baton Rouge Advocate,* December 8, 2000)
- "(Assistant Boy Scout leader) gets 45 years for a decade of sex abuse" (*Des Moines Register,* October 31, 2000)
- "Staffer accused of molesting boy scouts" (NewsMax.com, August 31, 2000), regarding an Oklahoma ex-Scout troop leader being sentenced to two hundred years in prison
- "Ex-scout leader faces charge of molesting boy 41 years ago" (*Washington Times,* March 18, 2000)[25]

Another search of fifty of America's largest newspapers by the Family Research Institute between 1989 and 2001 revealed 1,731 reports of sexual molestation involving 1,981 perpetrators and 5,253 victims. Many of the cited examples involved the Boy Scouts and other youth programs.[26] One case surveyed by FRI was the largest child molestation case in the history of Massachusetts involving Scoutmaster Christopher Reardon who was convicted in 2001 on seventy-five counts of rape, molestation, and dissemination of pornography involving twenty-nine boys.[27]

Though the Boy Scouts do not publicly correlate homosexuality with pedophilia, perhaps equally as important as simply banning homosexuals as Scoutmasters, the Boy Scouts have made a concerted effort to root out all homosexual abuse within its ranks. But it was only in the mid-1980s, long after the public Scoutmaster sex abuse scandals had begun, that the BSA began to take action. The BSA Statement on Child Abuse released in 1985 stated, "Sexual abuse of children is a fact in our society and a matter of great concern for most parents throughout our country. The BSA shares this concern."[28] The BSA did not actually admit to having a problem in its own ranks. What actually forced the Scouts to attack their own problem directly was a combination of the 1980s liability crisis when lawsuit awards were inflated and society became increasingly litigious and skyrocketing of insurance rates. The Scouts began raising an annual insurance fee of twenty dollars per troop in 1986.[29]

Until the late 1980s, the Boy Scouts settled sex abuse lawsuit cases out of court; but in 1987, the BSA was sued because Oregon Scoutmaster William Tobiassen allegedly abused one boy more than forty times. The Scouts were taken to task for not screening volunteers like Tobiassen as effectively as they should, and the Scouts had to fight desperately against a $10 million lawsuit.[30] In the end, the Boy Scouts paid $2.5 million.[31] Also in 1987, the parents of sixteen-year-old Brett Corbitt of Virginia filed a $30 million lawsuit against the BSA for a long-term sexual relationship that occurred between Corbitt and his Scoutmaster, Carl Bittenbender.[32] Between 1984 and 1992, the Boy Scouts of America were sued at least sixty times by families of Scouts abused by leaders, resulting in settlements of more than $16 million.[33]

A September 1986 *Scouting* magazine story titled "Child Abuse: A Critical Issue in Our Society" mentioned the importance of avoiding abuse in the BSA.[34] A similar article appeared in *Boys' Life* magazine that same month.[35] Shortly thereafter, the Boy Scouts hired veteran child abuse expert John Patterson to head up its efforts to improve antiabuse programs.[36] Under Patterson's direction, the BSA issued a 1988 pamphlet for local executives titled *Boy Scouts of America Background Information on Sex Abuse,* announcing that the organization had decided to take "bold, aggressive measures to combat the problem."[37] In 1989, the BSA revised its volunteer application to require references and asking questions about crime and child abuse.[38] The following year, the BSA released a ninety-minute video for Scouts called *A Time to Tell,* exposing child abuse and emphasizing: "recognize, resist, report."

Some sex abuse experts called the video the best device they'd
seen for teaching children about molestation.[39]

Today, Scouts and Scoutmasters are not allowed to sleep in
the same tents, and camps require adults and youth to observe
separate hours of use for the showers. The Boy Scout handbook is
explicit in instructing boys about how to avoid and report sexual
abuse. And beginning in 2002, extensive criminal background
checks were begun to screen new Scoutmasters.[40]

SADLY, OTHER youth organizations like the Girl Scouts, the
YMCA and the YWCA and the British Scouts (see chap. 13) have
yielded to pressure to allow openly homosexual adults as members. Beginning in 2002, the Big Brothers Big Sisters began allowing homosexuals to volunteer with the group as one-on-one
youth mentors. The organization does not even require parental
consent for school children to be placed with openly homosexual
mentors.[41]

Even before the Big Brothers' decision to allow openly homosexual mentors, a Family Research Institute study of reported
child molestation between 1989 and 2001 revealed that "a boy
in the Big Brothers program was about 5 times more likely to be
molested than was a Boy Scout."[42]

Today, Big Brothers Big Sisters of America is facing a constant barrage of pressure from concerned parents and educators
to reverse its policy or at least to require parental consent for the
placement of a child with a homosexual mentor. After the policy change last year, one local BBBSA chapter claimed to have
received twenty thousand protesting e-mails in one day. Another
local chapter executive director said, "Nearly 100 percent of the
people who called us about this policy said, 'We don't want this.'"[43]
According to World magazine, at least twelve local BBBSA executive directors have refused to implement the new policy permitting homosexual mentors without parental consent.[44]

Of course, like the Boy Scouts, Big Brothers Big Sisters is a
private organization that has the right to set its own policies. But
Americans have the right not to participate in an organization that

openly embraces the culture of immorality and scorns the authority of parents.

The future of American civic virtue and of the family itself is at stake in this fight for parental rights and moral decency. Big Brothers Big Sisters is involved in thousands of schools across America, and it will become—like the Boy Scouts should it, too, give in someday—the vehicle for the destruction of thousands of young lives.

CHAPTER 7

★★

The Right
to Be Virtuous

I am often asked why homosexuals don't start their own youth organization. There have been small, unsuccessful attempts, such as when the Queer Scouts organization in San Francisco tried to fill Bay Area Scoutmaster positions with homosexuals in the early 1990s. And William Boyce's homosexual grandson, William Mueller, founded Forgotten Scouts in San Francisco in 1991 to "counter the Boy Scouts' belief that gay men are somehow at odds with family values."[1] But the homosexual movement has generally refused to play by the rules of private association; Queer Scouts and Forgotten Scouts no longer exist, but the offensive movement to destroy the Boy Scouts is more aggressive than ever. Homosexuals have become part of a political and social agenda that will stop at nothing short of complete acceptance and equality in every corner of American society.

In order to achieve that lofty goal, homosexual activists and legal groups have taken liberal advantage of the litigious spirit sweeping America. In its larger context, it is a battle between judicial relativism (moral relativism and the judiciary combined) and constitutionalism. And leading the way has been the American Civil Liberties Union, amassing power and wealth unlike any other legal force in the nation. That the ACLU has picked a fight for freedom is undisputed; that the ACLU has done so with the intention of advancing ordered liberty and moral duty ought to raise serious doubt.

Author William Donohue has documented the ACLU's roots and early ties to the Communist Party in his books *The Politics of the American Civil Liberties Union* and *Twilight of Liberty: The Legacy of the ACLU*. Over the years, the ACLU broke ties with communism, but it has not abandoned its agenda for radical social change. Today, it operates as America's most ardent force for absolute social equality.

Neo-Nazis, Klansmen, and militant homosexual organizations have been among the odd clients of the ACLU. With a corps of powerhouse lawyers in fields ranging from estate planning to the environment, divorce law to criminal law, the ACLU has effectively become the single most powerful force in the American judiciary. In the more than five thousand cases that it argues annually, the ACLU claims the mantle of patriotic freedom—loving Americans. Yet the ACLU has declared all-out war on the Boy Scouts of America. Does the ACLU stand for liberty, or do the Boy Scouts stand for liberty?

This war against the Boy Scouts by the ACLU and its allies on the radical Left is not new. When West and Baden-Powell traveled to Portland, Oregon, to speak at a Boy Scout rally in the early days of Scouting, the socialist International Workers of the World staged a protest and booed the Scouting leaders off the podium.[2] And in the 1920s, the national secretary of the Young Communist League told Baden-Powell that the war between youth groups was a winner-take-all fight. Baden-Powell replied, "You can't fight without two. Our aim is to help the poorer boy, independent of all political questions, to get his fair chance of happiness and success in life."[3] In other words, the Boy Scouts have a mission independent of political ideology. And the Boy Scouts have no intention of being a political organization.

Even today, BSA maintains the same apolitical stance. According to BSA spokesman Gregg Shields, "We are an entirely apolitical organization, so we don't take positions, pro or con, on House bills, Senate bills or local legislation, even when it might directly affect us."[4] It's good the Boy Scouts make an effort to steer clear of politics, but they have been dragged into a political and cultural debate in which they have no choice but to contend against the likes of the ACLU. Whether we like it or not, the Boy Scouts have been politicized.

This is the America we live in today. But America has faced other challenges in the past: slavery, fascism, and communism. The Boy Scouts have been around to help fight the latter two struggles, and the Scouts are called by necessity to fight the moral wars of our own time.

In the early days of Scouting, James West had to confront a spreading communist agenda, and he did so by portraying communism as the archenemy of the Boy Scouts. "Neglected boyhood breeds bolshevism," he announced in a recruitment effort. And when the Boy Scouts of America went to Europe to participate in the 1920 World Jamboree, West declared that the international Scouting movement was a dike "against the rising tide of Bolshevism."[5]

We don't speak of communism and Bolshevism much anymore, but the ACLU has taken up much of the egalitarian idealism that gave birth to the communist idea. It is a stark contrast to the Boy Scouts of America, a difference illustrated by William Donohue. "At one level, the organizations have something in common: they are private, draw heavily on volunteers, and promote freedom. Their overarching difference is in their understanding of freedom."[6] Donohue pointed out the ACLU promotes freedom without responsibility, while duty is central to the message of Scouting.

And what is freedom? Either it comes from government, or it comes from God and is best maintained by keeping government minimal. The future of America rests on our capacity to decide between the two definitions of freedom. If we choose the ACLU, we might be freed in a certain sense without the moral restraints and responsibilities incumbent on people who hope to remain free, and in the course of time, we will be enslaved by our own lasciviousness. If we choose the Boy Scouts, we take on ourselves great responsibilities and commit to great sacrifice, but in so doing we will preserve our constitution, liberty, and way of life.

"If our civil liberties are ever destroyed in this country," said Midge Decter, "it won't be by boys taking oaths, but rather by people intent on stretching the delicate and complex social fabric of this free society beyond its breaking point."[7]

BY THE 1970s, America was moving toward the breaking point. It was in a haze of moral and legal confusion that eleven-year-old James Dale joined a Cub Scout pack in New Jersey in 1978. Dale worked his way through the ranks and became an Eagle Scout.

James Dale graduated from high school and entered Rutgers University in 1989. Following his freshman year, Dale became close friends with a homosexual man. "He told me about the gay community. That gave me the self-respect and pride I needed so that when I went back to Rutgers in my sophomore year, I had no problem telling other people," said Dale.[8] Dale's decision to come out would change the face of American culture forever.

At the start of his sophomore year, Dale joined a campus homosexual pride club called Lesbian and Gay Alliance. After only three months, Dale was elected president of the Rutgers group. Dale began to work with activists in the homosexual movement to promote its radical agenda. As Dale worked with LGA, he also served as an assistant Scoutmaster of a more traditional organization called Boy Scout Troop 73 of Matawan, New Jersey.[9]

In July 1990, Dale was a guest speaker at a conference for social workers and was featured in a local newspaper for his role in the conference. Leaders of the Monmouth Council where Dale served as assistant Scoutmaster took note of his public activism, and the council, led by Scout executive James W. Kay, was faced with telling James Dale that his lifestyle was not compatible with the principles outlined in Scouting. It was surely a difficult letter to write.

Of course, it was not the only case involving homosexuality the Boy Scouts were dealing with at the time. Timothy Curran had sued the Boy Scouts in California for excluding him under similar circumstances as Dale.

In an effort to publicly reiterate their position on homosexuality, the Boy Scouts of America released a public statement in 1991, explaining the basis in the oath and law for excluding homosexual leaders and members.[10] But the BSA position statement only emboldened Lambda in its efforts to manipulate the legal system to reinstate James Dale as a troop leader. On July 29, 1992, Lambda consulted with the firm of Cleary, Gottlieb, Steen, and Hamilton to file a lawsuit against the Monmouth Council. The lawsuit claimed that Dale had been discriminated against according to the New Jersey antidiscrimination law that had recently been amended to include "sexual orientation" as a protected minority.

The important legal question facing the Boy Scouts, in the Dale case as in Curran and other important cases, was whether or not the Scouts could be subject to the regulatory authority of government. Following the civil rights movement, state and federal legislators passed laws stating that commercial businesses were required to accommodate racial minorities and women. Initially, these laws were an important step toward equality in American society.

Over time, public accommodation laws have been expanded to cover additional categories of minorities such as veteran status, disability, or sexual orientation. And in the 1980s, the Supreme Court ruled that men-only civic business organizations like the Rotary and the Jaycees had to include women in their memberships. Excluding women could put them at a disadvantage for employment decisions and business transactions, the court reasoned.

But laws of public accommodation don't apply to everyone and everything everywhere. Unlike the business-oriented Rotary and Jaycees, the Boy Scouts is a youth education organization dedicated to certain principles of honor (remember that honor requires exclusivity). Likewise, churches are private institutions built on sets of beliefs only certain people can adhere to.

On November 5, 1995, Superior Court Judge Patrick McGann ruled that the Boy Scouts are exempt from the New Jersey antidiscrimination laws. Clearly understanding the growing legal problem of the homosexual movement for private groups like the Boy Scouts, McGann declared, "Men who do those criminal and immoral acts cannot be held out as role models."[11]

Dale and Lambda appealed. On March 2, 1998, an intermediate appeals court reversed McGann's decision. For the majority in the 2–1 decision, Judge James Havey argued that the Scouts had wrongfully discriminated against Dale. Homosexuals, Havey claimed, could only be considered threats to Scouting if they purposefully and blatantly undermined the Scout oath and law.[12]

This time, the Boy Scouts appealed Havey's ruling to the New Jersey State Supreme Court. On January 5, 1999, New Jersey's high court heard arguments from Dale's attorney Evan Wolfson and Boy Scouts of America attorney George Davidson. In a friend-of-the-court brief filed by the Claremont Institute on behalf of the Scouts, Philip J. Griego wrote: "The issue is whether the Boy Scouts of America shall retain the liberty, guaranteed by the First Amendment, to define its own identity, to apply its own creed to express the traditional moral point of view that homosexuality is neither moral nor reverent. Or, shall New Jersey require them to include among their leadership members whose avowed purpose is to impart a message their leadership does not wish to convey?"[13] The Claremont brief went on to explain several key points. First, freedom of association is central to America's sense of freedom. Within that right lies the primary manner by which citizens are able to build strength behind a cause, worship together at church, and spread ideas. Second, if the court were to deny the Scouts and other organizations the ability to set their

own membership standards, it would destroy the essence of freedom of association for the state of New Jersey. Finally, the initial
decision of Judge McGann was the correct decision, and there
was no reason to doubt his sense of judgment.

On August 4, 1999, the majority decision was released. It was
unanimous, 7–0. Chief Justice Deborah T. Portiz authored the
comprehensive, eighty-nine-page, thirty-thousand-word decision
about her theory of tolerance. Portiz opined, "The sad truth is
that excluded groups and individuals have been prevented from
full participation in the social, economic, and political life of our
country. . . . Adherence to the principles of equality demands that
our legal system protect the victims of invidious discrimination."[14]
Portiz assumed all discrimination is evil, while, in fact, her court
decision itself was a form of discrimination in favor of one liti-
gant over another. Discrimination is implied in any choice made
by human beings, and unless Portiz could make the case that the
Scouts were a public accommodation, her ramblings on discrimination and tolerance would be legally baseless.

Instead of basing her decision on the New Jersey Constitution
or other state law, Portiz took hold of the Scout oath and law and
wrung them dry of meaning: "Exclusion of members solely on the
basis of their sexual orientation is inconsistent with Boy Scouts'
commitment to a diverse and 'representative' membership [and]
contradicts Boy Scouts' overarching objective to reach 'all eligible
youth.' Boy Scout members do not associate for the purpose of disseminating the belief that homosexuality is immoral; Boy Scouts
discourages its leaders from disseminating any views on sexual
issues; and Boy Scouts includes sponsors and members who subscribe to different views in respect to homosexuality."[15]

Portiz was correct in her ruling when she stated that the Boy
Scouts do not associate for the purpose of "disseminating the belief that homosexuality is immoral" but have other concerns that
are spoken of much more openly among the rank and file, such as
camping and hiking and earning merit badges. And the fact that
opposition to homosexuality is not the most important detail of
the Scouting program is hardly a basis for concluding, with the co-

ercive force of the law, that the Boy Scouts must suddenly include homosexuals. The Scout oath and law condemn homosexuality implicitly, and official Scout policy does so explicitly, according to the organization that created and maintains those creeds. But Judge Portiz thought she knew the meaning of the Scout oath and law better than the Scouts themselves.

Instead of deciding the issue strictly on the objective grounds of public accommodation laws, Portiz set out to forcefully interpret the Boy Scout oath and law on behalf of the Scouts. Portiz discarded the BSA's attempts to distinguish between immoral choices and genuine diversity. But even if there had been a contradiction in the BSA's positions on diversity, what authority did the New Jersey Supreme Court have to force the Scouts to admit homosexuals?

The court didn't even address the issue of its own authority to decide the meaning of the Scout oath and law. It was simply assumed. The court utterly ignored the fundamental distinction between public accommodation and private association. Public accommodation refers to property to which the public does or should have general access, meaning it should actively accommodate any who are law abiding citizens willing to pay the same price of entry their fellow citizens would pay. Private association, on the other hand, like private property, is subject to the control of the private owner. But according to the New Jersey Supreme Court, the Boy Scouts were no longer a private organization.

THE ISSUE OF private association is generally independent of ideology and belief. I'm not afraid to defend the Boy Scouts for having a good policy regulating its membership, but whether the policy is good or bad, so-called liberals also should recognize the liberty of the Boy Scouts to maintain their own standards, independent of government coercion. The issue affects liberals as well as conservatives, Scouting for All as well as the Boy Scouts of America.

Even the ACLU has litigated, frequently, for the freedom of association, and it certainly maintains a public position of support for that right. A 1952 ACLU policy statement recognized the right of business owners to deny access to any group they wish, and a 1972 policy read, "Private associations and organizations, as such, lie beyond the legitimate concern of the state and are constitutionally protected against governmental interference. The freedom of association guaranteed by the First Amendment insulates individuals in these private activities." The problem is that the ACLU and its left-wing allies use these principles selectively. When supposed individual entitlements appear to be more important than constitutionally protected free association, the ACLU has taken the radically individualistic position. While the ACLU has made enthusiastic defense of marginal extremist groups like the Ku Klux Klan and neo-Nazis, it has stood against the right of Grove City College in Pennsylvania and Hillsdale College in Michigan to have autonomy over their admissions and financial policies without regulation by the federal government. In 1983, the ACLU sued a Pennsylvania Catholic youth center for refusing to allow rock singer Ozzy Osbourne to perform at a youth event.[16]

Here again for the Boy Scouts, individual "entitlements" triumphed over constitutional rights. William Donohue observed, "What is most interesting about the ACLU's approach to the Boy Scouts is its determination to contract the private sphere and expand the public domain. With few exceptions, the ACLU seeks to lengthen the arms of government by narrowing what constitutes the private orbit, often by reinterpreting the criteria on which private associations are based."[17]

In the *Wall Street Journal*, Richard Sincere of the Independent Gay Forum outlined three reasons the New Jersey *Dale* decision was a setback for the autonomy of private organizations, including homosexual groups. First, said Sincere, the decision eroded freedom of association. Second, it further expanded the definition of what is public at the expense of what is private. Third, while the court's written opinion offered a strong argument for why the Boy Scouts should voluntarily change their policy, it failed to demonstrate why the government should force them to do so.[18]

In the name of civil rights, the Supreme Court of New Jersey damaged civil rights for all. Freedom of association was tarnished, and in the words of one columnist, "New Jersey is well on the road to fascism."[19]

THE DAY OF the New Jersey Supreme Court decision, the Boy Scouts of America announced an appeal to the U.S. Supreme Court, a body that hears few state appeal cases. But because the California Supreme Court had ruled in the Curran case and the James Randall case (alleging discrimination against atheists, see chap. 11) that the Scouts have the right to set their own membership standards, a hearing on the issue was not unlikely in the nation's high court.

On January 10, 2000, the Supreme Court agreed to review the New Jersey case. The BSA submitted a case on February 29 with twenty-one other organizations filing friend-of-the-court briefings in support of the BSA, including the American Center for Law and Justice, the Association of American Physicians and Surgeons, the Cato Institute, the Center for Individual Rights, the Claremont Institute, the Eagle Forum Education and Legal Defense Fund, Focus on the Family, the Independent Women's Forum, the Southeast Legal Foundation, the Southern Baptist Convention, and the Texas Justice Foundation.[20] Even Gays and Lesbians for Individual Liberty filed a brief on the side of the Scouts, fearing that a decision against private autonomy would mean a judge could then have the precedence to quash homosexual organizations.[21]

The ACLU Lesbian and Gay Rights Project and Lambda joined many organizations in filing the largest friend-of-the-court briefing on an issue of this nature in history. These groups included the Mexican-American Legal Defense and Educational Fund, the National Association for the Advancement of Colored People Legal Defense and Educational Fund, the National Asian-Pacific Legal Consortium, the National Council of Jewish Women, the American Federation of Teachers, the Anti-Defamation League, the California Women's Law Center, the Center for Women Policy Studies, Equal Rights Advocates, the Human Rights Campaign, the National Gay and Lesbian Task Force, the National Association of Women Legal Defense and Educational Fund, the National Partnership for Women and Families, the National Women's Law Center, People for the American Way Foundation, Women Employed, and the Women's Law Project.[22] A total of thirty-seven amici briefs were submitted, making it, according to law Professor Joseph D. Kearney of Marquette University, one of the ten largest Supreme Court cases (as measured by amici filings) in history.[23]

A GREAT MORAL DIVIDE was on display outside the U.S. Supreme Court building in the early morning hours of Wednesday, April 26, 2000. Homosexual activists and evangelical Christians, lawyers and newspaper reporters, television cameramen and magazine photographers, policemen and former Boy Scouts all mixed together along the wide street and sidewalks that separate Congress from the Supreme Court. As the sun rose in the crisp Washington sky, both George Davidson and Evan Wolfson felt the pressure. One sought to knock down an organization, another to preserve the very foundations on which American liberty and justice rest.

A car drove up to the crowded sidewalk, and out stepped Wolfson with James Dale. They slowly made their way through the crowds. Both wore elegant suits; Dale was trim and tanned. The crowd cheered and booed as the Lambda legal team escorted Dale to the heavy doors.

Another car arrived, and Davidson stepped out. He walked up to the doors in the same crowd Wolfson and Dale had gone through. The voices exchanged their cheers to boos, or their boos to cheers. The reporters asked questions.

Moments later, George Davidson stood before the robed court. The issue was simple, he said. "This case is about the freedom of a voluntary association to choose its own leaders."[24] He said that government has no business coercing a private group to accept standards that contradict the group's core mission.

When it was Evan Wolfson's turn, Justice Anthony Kennedy asked, "Who is better qualified to determine the expressive purpose of the Boy Scouts—the Boy Scouts or the New Jersey Supreme

Court?"[25] Steven Breyer followed up: "In your view, a Catholic organization has to admit Jews, and a Jewish organization has to admit Catholics."[26]

TWO MONTHS and two days later was judgment day. The court was unpredictable, and pundits predicted a close vote. Five years before, the U.S. Supreme Court upheld the right of sponsors of New York's Saint Patrick's Day parade to exclude homosexuals from participation. In a rare moment, the ACLU had actually come to the defense of the Ancient Order of Hibernians, the organizers of the parade, in its right to discriminate against the Irish Lesbian and Gay Organization. But in the 1980s, the Supreme Court had narrowed the legal definition of public accommodation by ruling that the Jaycees and Rotary as business-oriented organizations (as opposed to moral or educational organizations like the BSA) had to admit women into their membership.[27]

In the case of *Boy Scouts of America v. Dale,* by a vote of 5–4, the U.S. Supreme Court upheld the right of the Boy Scouts and all private organizations to choose their own standards of membership. In the majority opinion, Chief Justice William Rehnquist concluded, "The presence of Dale as an assistant scoutmaster would . . . surely interfere with the Boy Scouts' choice not to propound a point of view contrary to its beliefs."[28]

On behalf of the four dissenting justices, Justice Anthony Stevens, like Judge Portiz in New Jersey, took the liberty of interpreting the Scout oath and law for himself in a desperate effort to prove the Boy Scouts' opposition to homosexuality is not central to the Scouts' existence and therefore not a necessary position to maintain. "It is plain as the light of day," Stevens wrote, "that neither one of these principles, 'morally straight' and 'clean,' says the slightest thing about homosexuality. Indeed, neither term in the Boy Scouts' law and oath expresses any position whatsoever on sexual matters. BSA's mission statement and federal charter say nothing on the matter; its official membership policy is silent; its scout oath and law and accompanying definitions are devoid of any view on the topic."[29]

Chief Justice Rehnquist responded to Stevens's bold critique of the Scout oath and law with three points:

First, associations do not have to associate for the "purpose" of disseminating a certain message in order to be entitled to the protections of the First Amendment. Second, even if the Boy Scouts discourages Scout leaders from disseminating views on sexual issues, a fact that the Boy Scouts disputes with contrary evidence, the First Amendment protects the Boy Scouts' method of statement. Third, the First Amendment simply does not require that every member of a group agree on every issue in order for the group's policy to be "expressive association." The Boy Scouts takes an official position with respect to homosexual conduct, and that is sufficient for First Amendment purposes. The fact that the organization does not trumpet its views from the housetops, or that it tolerates dissent within its ranks, does not mean that its views receive no First Amendment protection.[30]

The court made it clear that free association is a fundamental right protected by the First Amendment. The Supreme Court scored a major victory for churches and organizations of all shapes, sizes, colors, and purposes, not the least of which is the powerful network of organizations that compose the homosexual front.

Thanks to the First Amendment, an organization can limit its membership to women, as the civic Philanthropic Educational Organization has done. It can limit its membership to ancestors of American patriots, as the Sons and Daughters of the American Revolution have done. It can limit its membership to those who have passed the test, achieved the goal, inherited the wealth, earned the money, paid the dues, and affirmed the truths.

CHAPTER 8

★★

Struggle for the Soul of the Boy Scouts

The summer of the *Dale* decision, Boy Scout Troop 174 trekked across Washington State's Cascade Mountains through the Mount Baker/Snoqualmie National Forest, covering some of God's most splendid, untouched creation. It was a grand week in the midst of nature at its essence. It was the only fifty-miler I've been on that was spared the predicament of rain, so we slept under the stars every night except for the miserable night at Lyman Lake when the mosquitoes were so bad we barely survived the experience of putting up our tents and crawling inside.

After we completed the hike on a warm Sunday morning, I led "church" outside an old pioneer cabin at Agnes Creek Trailhead. I read from Ezekiel 33, reflecting on the Boy Scout motto to be prepared. "However, if the watchman sees the sword coming but doesn't blow the trumpet, so that the people aren't warned, and the sword comes and takes away their lives, then they have been taken away because of their iniquity, but I will hold the watchman accountable for their blood" (v. 6). Then we had group prayer, mostly thanksgiving for an excellent week of fellowship and safe hiking. An old-fashioned tour bus picked us up at the trailhead, gear and all, and we traversed the dusty dirt roads all the way to downtown Stehekin, Washington.

After arriving at a campground near the edge of the pier, we set down our bags and dove off the wharf into the cool waters of

Lake Chelan for a refreshing swim. That evening consisted of several dozen rounds of Troop 174's trademark card game: kings and peasants.

Before heading to bed, I hung my food and "smellables" in the bear bag up the rocky hill from our campsite. Then I settled into my sleeping bag on the uncomfortable, sloping ground, listening to the joking chatter of Mike and Drew as they roped up their bear bags. Everyone else was half-asleep.

"Rattlesnake!" Mike yelled suddenly, leaping back from the bear-bag area.

One never knows how quickly he can be awakened until he hears that word shouted from several yards away. Flashlights clicked on, and eyes turned toward the hissing, writhing reptile.

And the assistant Scoutmaster, Cameron, already had his big-blade knife out of his hip pocket by the time Mike uttered the second syllable. Cameron had been prepared for this sort of thing all week. After Cameron's father died in the late 1980s, my grandpa, Ed, and Scoutmaster Doug sustained Cameron and inspired him to continue in school and life. Cameron joined the Marine Corps and spent years on duty for the first President Bush at Camp David. He later became a sheriff's deputy in King County, Washington, before rejoining the Marines to fight the War on Terror.

But for now, Cameron was leading the War on Rattlesnakes.

In a few motions, Cameron grabbed both of Derek's ski poles and proceeded toward the vile creature. "Don't move," he commanded, with all eyes fixed on him and the rattlesnake. The western diamondback coiled and reared its venomous head toward Cameron, who mechanically pinned the head between the two ski poles. With the knife, he quickly reached down toward the snake and in one swift motion sliced off its head.

As nerves calmed, the snake continued rattling for a minute or two, and we stood around celebrating its funeral. Cameron finished his task by cutting the rattle from the snake's tail, a gift later strung into an Indian-craft necklace for Scoutmaster Doug. Then, Mike and Drew were given the distinction of carrying the dead reptile (by its tail of course) to the outhouse at the edge of the campground.

Needless to say, getting to sleep that night was a bit of a challenge, particularly as we had been briefed by Cameron earlier in the week about the dangers of snakes crawling into sleeping bags. Somehow, we all woke up the next morning alive.

BUT THE BIGGEST viper of all was not dead; the serpent of cultural terrorism was just commencing its attack on America. And as al-Qaeda struck at our greatest buildings on September 11, 2001, so the radical Left slithered into the camp of America's defining cultural institution: the Boy Scouts of America.

Following the *Dale* decision, practically every left-wing group and power broker in America sent in battalions of troops to wage war on the Boy Scouts. A mountain of press release statements rolled off faxes and onto e-mail servers and Web sites on June 28, 2000. Joint press conferences were held, James Dale was enlisted by Keppler Associates Speakers Bureau to become a celebrity speaker, and ACLU lawyers plotted their next attacks. "Victory could prove costly," wrote David Crary of the Associated Press. "Critics say that the Boy Scouts have squandered a reputation for tolerance and face an erosion of public support."[1]

Public support for Scouting has not declined as much as the Left would like. One year after the *Dale* decision, a poll in *Newsweek* magazine showed that 70 percent of Scouting parents approve of the Boy Scouts' ban on homosexuals and atheists, and 30 percent disagree and believe the Scouts should become more inclusive.[2]

The August 6, 2001, issue of *Newsweek* that featured the poll, showed on its cover a rather somber looking Boy Scout with the headline, "The Struggle for the Soul of the Boy Scouts." As the feature stories unfolded, *Newsweek* portrayed the BSA as a dwindling organization, with little hope if it refuses to give in. When the magazine claimed that the Scouts' membership had fallen by various amounts in different regions around the country, the BSA refuted *Newsweek*'s bias by claiming that the 2.2 percent decrease in membership from 1999 to 2000 could most accurately be traced to a lesser number of elementary school children compared to statistics from the early and mid-1990s.

While a connection between erosion of public support for Scouting and smaller membership is thus far questionable, attacking the Boy Scouts has become something of a fad among the leftist elites since 2000.

When Japanese Girl and Boy Scouts visited Berkeley, California, on a goodwill mission, a homosexual city council member pressured the city to cancel a reception for the Scouts, saying that such a reception would be an endorsement of the Boy Scouts of America and its policy banning homosexuals. Interestingly, the Girl and Boy Scouts of Japan did not even have a policy on homosexuals.[3]

The nation's most radical animal rights organization searched the list of Scouting's available merit badges to identify a merit badge to lobby against. People for the Ethical Treatment of Animals (PETA) discovered that fishing and fish and wildlife management merit badges teach "young people that hooking, maiming, suffocating, and killing is acceptable."[4] PETA paid for television advertisements in Connecticut and Texas, starring young animal rights activist Justin Aligata. BSA practices the "catch and release" method in fishing, which the Catch and Release Foundation says begins for children "the process of discovery and awareness that leads to an understanding of . . . the importance of man's wise stewardship of his environment."[5] But PETA claimed, "It is something that the fish would clearly rather not go through."[6]

Left-wing public servants began saying things about the Boy Scouts that would have led to their impeachment, recall, or pressured resignation just a few decades ago. At a homosexual rally in Maryland in July 2000, Maryland Governor Parris Glendening asserted that the BSA homosexual policy is "outrageous and divisive."[7] Washington Governor Gary Locke, in a letter of support to a Scouting for All Gay Scouts and All Gay Youth Week rally in Seattle, wrote, "I applaud your organization's efforts to make scouting accessible to all youth. . . . We owe a debt of gratitude to organizations such as yours that strive to foster an increased awareness and appreciation of the richness and depth of our diversity."[8]

Asked by the *Seattle Gay News* to expand on his anti-Scout position, Locke replied, "The Boy Scouts of America is doing a great disservice to young people. These young men are feeling isolated, ostracized and looking for companionship and leadership. These young men should be embraced by the Boy Scouts, but they're not and it's absolutely wrong."[9]

The political party of Gary Locke and Parris Glendening was no more supportive of Scouting at the 2000 Democratic Convention in Los Angeles. Convention organizers brought in six Eagle Scouts representing the Los Angeles BSA Council to lead the flag ceremony on the final evening of the convention. Gloria Johnson, a delegate from California who learned that Scouts would be on duty, mobilized several other delegates to help create signs reading "We Support Gay Scouts."[10]

As the nation watched on television, the Scouts emerged from backstage in full uniform. Some of the crowd cheered, and from the front, a distinctive booing began. The booing grew louder, and Gloria Johnson's signs became visible in the crowded arena. Party officials refused to apologize for the poor reception of the Scouts. Rick Hess, a spokesman for the Democratic National Committee, declared, "Democrats across the board support equal rights for gays and lesbians and we want to make sure that they aren't discriminated against."[11]

Hypocritically, the Democratic Party of California had argued before the U.S. Supreme Court, at about the same time as the *Dale* case, that it had the right to a closed primary election system in order to limit its political association. As with *Dale,* the high court ruled in *Democratic Party v. Jones* that a state's interests are less important than a private political party's right to exclude members.[12] But the Democrats cared little about the Boy Scouts' right to exclude. Valerie Richardson wrote in the *Washington Times,* "Support for homosexual rights has become an integral part of the Democratic orthodoxy, as unassailable as the party's pro-choice or civil rights planks. Since the Supreme Court ruled that the Boy Scouts can ban homosexual leaders, the Democrats have sided squarely with homosexuals in condemning the decision."[13]

SIX DAYS AFTER the convention incident, the Gay and Lesbian Alliance Against Defamation, the ACLU, and other groups declared August 21 a National Day of Protest, planning demonstrations at the Boy Scouts of America national headquarters in Irving, Texas, and at thirty-six local council offices in twenty-one states. Interestingly, many of the thirty-six councils reported that no protests took place. Where protests occurred, only handfuls of people participated.[14]

The demonstrators who did take time off their jobs presented petition signatures to local Scouting officials, demanding the admission of homosexuals and atheists in the Boy Scouts. Protesters around the country carried signs featuring words like "bigot," "tolerance," and "human rights."

In San Diego, four protestors led by Howard Mezner showed up at the Desert Pacific Council. Mezner said he encouraged the Scouts to embrace openly homosexual Scoutmasters. He said that such an individual is a "man of the community who's working as part of a family. It can be two men. It can be two women. Society is changing. Times are changing. Boy Scouts need to keep up with times." Mezner explained that his objective in protesting the BSA was to "take it back from the Christian, fundamentalist right."[15]

THE MOST VOCAL participant during the protest day was a small grassroots organization called Scouting for All. It was founded in 1997 by Scott Cozza, a psychologist and left-wing activist from Petaluma, California, and a former San Francisco Bay Area Scoutmaster named Dave Rice whose militant activism in the homosexual movement led to his dismissal from Scouting. Cozza and Rice launched a nonprofit action organization called Scouting for All dedicated to gathering petition signatures against the Scouts.

Around the same time Cozza cofounded Scouting for All, he sent his eleven-year-old son Steven to join a local Boy Scout troop.

Steven made his debut as the Boy Scout who hates the Boy Scouts on December 27, 1997, when he wrote a letter to the editor of a local newspaper: "I am 12 years old and a Life rank Boy Scout. I want people to know that the Boy Scouts of America . . . won't allow gay kids or grown-ups in scouting. I hope to change this one bad thing about the Boy Scouts of America. I hope all of you who read this letter to the editor will also want to help me in my efforts by calling Scouting for All. . . . Gay kids should be allowed to be scouts. And I know kids who have gay dads would want their dads to be able to be an assistant scoutmaster like my dad."[16]

Steven Cozza worked to achieve his Eagle Scout Award while speaking at rallies and churches about the evils of the Scout oath and law. In 1999, Cozza achieved the rank of Eagle Scout at a ceremony in which he pledged: "I, Steven Cozza, believe in the Boy Scouts of America as a movement which has as its aim and purpose character building and citizenship training. I believe it to be a movement that helps a Scout become master of his own powers, helps him get along well with other people and helps him find a worthy use for his powers. I, therefore, believe it is my duty to do my best to obey the Scout oath and law. I hereby renew my faith in Scouting and promise to do what I can in service to other Scouts who have not come this far along the Eagle trail."[17] On taking the Eagle Scout pledge, Steven immediately violated his sworn vow to renew his faith in Scouting by mailing his Eagle badge back to the BSA national headquarters and publicly asking for other "fair-minded Scouts to renounce their badges, which will be gathered and returned to the BSA."[18]

When I exchanged e-mails with Steven in late 2001, I asked him why he was so zealous in his opposition to the Boy Scouts. "When I found out the BSA discriminated against my friends," he wrote, "I couldn't live with myself if I stayed in scouting and didn't do anything about it. I felt the pain the BSA causes gays. I have a Christian camp counselor, Robert Espindola who taught me about God, family values, taking care of our environment and being moral. You know something. He is gay. I became sad and angry that the BSA would discriminate against my friend Robert."[19]

In a letter to Scouting for All members, Steven Cozza wrote that the BSA had been destroyed by "religious fundamentalists" because they "use the Scout Law and Scout Oath as weapons of hatred, discrimination, and bigotry to hurt people who are gay in the same way they use the Bible, Jesus Christ and God to hurt gay youth and adults. This type of behavior is what is immoral."[20]

SCOUTING FOR ALL is most famous for its role in the production of *A Scout's Honor,* a 2001 film profiling the "heroic" struggles of Timothy Curran, James Dale, David Rice, and Steven Cozza. *A Scout's Honor* was produced by homosexual activist Tom Shepard for Point of View productions, and its board of advisers included Kevin Jennings, executive director of Gay, Lesbian, and Straight Education Network (GLSEN).[21] The documentary wouldn't be so notable except that it was funded in part by taxpayers through the Independent Television Service, a subsidiary of PBS. "It's one thing if Shepard were to produce a film on his private dime," said Peter LaBarbera of the Culture and Family Institute. "But when you bring the taxpayer money in to undermine the Boy Scouts of America, it changes things. Then it becomes a concern of taxpaying Americans."[22]

After winning an audience award and the Freedom of Statement Award at the Sundance Film Festival, *A Scout's Honor* was screened at a May 2001 homosexual "Pridefest Celebration" in Philadelphia at which James Dale was a keynote speaker.[23]

Then, PBS decided to air *Scout's Honor* across America on taxpayer-funded television stations. Concerned Women for America, the American Family Association, and other conservative family policy organizations lobbied PBS to prevent the televising. On June 19, 2001, PBS aired the hour-long documentary.

Don Wildmon, president of the American Family Association, stated, "To trash the Boy Scouts is one thing, but to use taxpayer funds to do it is an outrage. Every taxpayer ought to contact his local PBS, and his congressman, and give him an earful."[24] Earfuls were given, and to this date PBS has denied equal time to the Boy Scouts of America. *Scout's Honor,* hailed by the homosexual movement as a masterpiece, has since been screened on hundreds of college campuses, by educational and community service organizations, and by churches.

WITH THE START of a new school year, Troop 174 meetings resumed the fall after the *Dale* decision and the fifty-mile hike in the Cascades. I was installed as senior patrol leader of Boy Scout Troop 174, and I was in charge of setting the troop meeting agendas each Monday night. One evening, I opened up the floor to a discussion about the controversies of the Boy Scouts of America.

I began by explaining the *Dale* decision and outlined a few of the recent attacks on Scouting. I was surprised to find that many of my fellow Scouts were generally unaware of the events unfolding. It's good some were oblivious, I reflected later on, for the matters troubling the Boy Scouts are a distraction from all the good things Scouting continues to do for America.

For most Scouts, the membership policies banning homosexuals seemed a no-brainer. One boy announced, "I wouldn't want to sleep in a tent with a gay guy!" A brief chuckle spread in the room. Another chimed in: "I don't see why gay people are so desperate to get involved in the Scouts. They should just start their own group."

On the other side of the argument, someone pointed out that if homosexuals aren't hurting anyone they should be allowed membership.

I learned there is not uniform agreement among the rank and file about the Boy Scouts' membership standards. Regardless, my fellow Scouts unanimously agreed that attacks on the Boy Scouts were obnoxious and denigrating.

CHAPTER 9

★★★

The Divided Way: United Way Deception

Nasty words about the Boy Scouts can go only so far to intimidate a rock-solid character-building organization. In fact, if the threats and jeers from the likes of the ACLU and Scouting for All had any impact at all, it was to steel the Boy Scouts' resolve to mentor young men and instill timeless virtues.

But a more important test comes with finances. Most notably, local chapters of America's largest charitable giving organization, the United Way, began to pull valuable funds from Boy Scout programs when local United Way nondiscrimination policies conflicted with the Scouts' policies banning homosexuals and atheists from leadership positions. Robert Carleson, an attorney and president of the Scouting Legal Defense Fund, suggests that it be very clear when we are dealing with *local* United Way chapters so as to avoid incorrectly offending the national United Way.

Shortly after the decision in *Boy Scouts of America v. Dale*, the United Way of Pierce County, Washington, began to discuss its relationship with organizations whose antidiscrimination codes conflicted with its own and amended its funding policy to state that general fund money would be disbursed only to organizations that do not discriminate on the basis of sexual orientation. United Way of Pierce County gave the affected groups two years to change their policies or face budget cuts.[1]

I called Rick Allen, the local United Way president, and I asked him about the policy changes. Allen insisted the change was not directed specifically at the Boy Scouts. Interestingly, the Boy Scouts was the only group affected.[2]

I then called Doug Dillow, executive for the Pacific Harbors Boy Scout Council, the council affected by the United Way funding change. Dillow told me, "It is going to be harder. We're going to have to find alternative sources of funding."[3]

Indeed, the United Way had been, until it decided to end its annual check to the Scouts, a steady and reliable source of funding for local Scouting programs.

Until July 2003—the cutoff point for the Pacific Harbors Scouts to give in on morals or give up on allocated United Way money—the United Way of Pierce County had allocated a sizable check to the Pacific Harbors Council of the Boy Scouts every July. United Way gave $74,000 to the Scouts in 2002, and the contribution had been as high as $100,000 in previous years.

The Boy Scouts once ranked high on the civic pedestal of communities across America. But those who would rather spit on the Boy Scouts exerted such intense pressure on the United Way that it withdrew its crucial general funds from Scouting in my local council. Suddenly, an old relationship came to an end.

THE 1910s and 1920s were times of great civic renewal and change. Rotary International was founded in 1905, Kiwanis in 1914, and Lions Club in 1917. World War I veterans founded the American Legion in 1919, and the Knights of Columbus and other religious fellowships appeared during the same era.[4] Each of the new civic membership organizations provided an outlet for business, religious, and community leaders to network and support worthy local causes. Each new organization sponsored Boy Scout troops.[5]

Civic organizations had to find a way to make charitable giving more efficient. The Boy Scouts of America, led by James West, took a particular interest in making it more convenient for donors to back the Scouts. So the BSA was one of a dozen service groups that cofounded the American Association of Community Organizations in 1918. The AACO soon became known as the United Way. Thanks in part to the partnership and assistance of the Boy Scouts of America, the United Way grew into a respected charitable clearinghouse to serve the burgeoning market of community service organizations.[6]

Since the 1950s, the United Way has been the single most important funding source for the Boy Scouts of America.[7] Like the Scouts, the United Way has been dedicated to helping other people at all times, to doing a good turn daily.

Until 1992. That's when Timothy Curran, the early 1990s poster boy of the anti-Scouts, encouraged San Francisco's United Way of the Bay Area (UWBA) to set a new antidiscrimination policy for the protection of lesbians, gays, bisexuals, and transgender people (LGBT). Without much hesitation, UWBA demanded the local Boy Scout council change its nondiscrimination policy so homosexuals could take part in troop activities.[8]

UWBA was and remains the largest private funding campaign for health and human services in Northern California, and thus the policy change affected hundreds of companies whose employees gave to Scouting through the United Way.[9] According to the UWBA Web site, the local United Way opposes the Boy Scouts because: "United Way of the Bay Area's non-discrimination policy reflects the values of inclusion and diversity. United Way of the Bay Area will not provide grants to any agency that cannot sign our non-discrimination policy which requires that an agency not deny service to a potential client or member on the basis of age, gender, race, sexual orientation, national origin, religion or presence of a disability. The Boy Scouts of America have not signed our non-discrimination policy."[10]

The Boy Scouts of America immediately responded to the San Francisco conflict by encouraging the San Francisco Scout council to resist the pressures of the United Way, declaring that homosexuality is a threat to the "values and principles" of Scouting. Even Jacques Moreillon, secretary general of the World Organization of the Scout Movement (WOSM), used the conflict to bring light to the international Scouting movement's commitment to character and traditional values. "Scouting actively discourages homosexuals from joining its ranks," said Moreillon. "We strongly believe that our Scout youth should not be a hunting ground for homosexuals."[11]

The Gay and Lesbian Alliance Against Defamation immediately lashed out against the international Scouting movement. "To participate in such a hateful dialogue is horribly irresponsible," said Los Angeles GLAAD director Chris Fowler. New York GLAAD executive Ellen Carton said, "We encourage the United Way to follow through with their proposal, and to withhold all funds allocated to the Boy Scouts until the policy is reversed. Furthermore, we challenge all United Way chapters across the country to follow the United Way San Francisco Bay Area's lead."[12]

Today, donors to the United Way Bay Area from six hundred Northern California employers and hundreds of foundations send their contributions, knowingly or unknowingly, to the radical homosexual front. Of the six major United Way Bay Area strategic partners, two represent the LGBT movement. The Horizons Foundation supports nonprofit organizations that serve homosexuals in "arts and culture, awareness, advocacy and civic rights, health and human services, children, youth and families." And Out and Equal Workplace Advocates funds homosexual causes that increase "networking, leadership, volunteerism, and philanthropy among LGBT people."[13]

SINCE GLAAD AND other prohomosexual rights organizations began lobbying United Way chapters to drop funding to the Scouts in 1992, many United Way chapters have given in. From 1993 through June 2000, eight major United Way chapters adopted antidiscrimination codes and ceased funding to the BSA: Santa Clara and Santa Cruz, California; New Haven and Branford, Connecticut; Santa Fe, New Mexico; Portland, Maine; and Somerset County, New Jersey.[14]

A week before the Supreme Court *Dale* decision, the United Way chapter in Providence, Rhode Island, adopted a new antidiscrimination policy to include homosexuals. The chapter sent a letter to the sixty-five recipients of its $7.3 million in funding, warning that any organizations that did not comply with the policy by January 2001 would be cut off. William Allen, executive vice president of community services, told newspapers that while the letter did not mention the BSA, the policy was intended specifically for the Scouts. "We concluded that it was time for the United Way . . . to act and to be a leader on this," Allen said.[15]

The day after the Supreme Court decision, the United Way of Central Massachusetts (UWCM) announced its intention to reconsider ties to the Mohegan BSA Council. In the previous year, the United Way had given more than $138,000 to the Scouts. "It's really something that we're going to have to take a look at now that the Supreme Court has handed down its decision," said Eric Buch, UWCM president.[16]

IN MOST COMMUNITIES, the United Way is still committed to the Boy Scouts. In 1996, the national United Way reported total contributions to the Boy Scouts of America were $83.7 million.[17] And in 1999, local United Ways gave more than $85 million to the Boy Scouts of America around the country.[18] Most of United Way's fourteen hundred chapters continue to fund the Boy Scouts, but the relationship is becoming increasingly unstable.

To date, nearly eighty United Way chapters have severed allocations to the Boy Scouts, which seems like a small fraction of fourteen hundred chapters. But the chapters that have cut funding tend to be in major cities where Scouting membership is highly concentrated and where Scouts desperately need funding.

Since the Boy Scouts are heavily dependent on the United Way for funding and the United Way is heavily dependent on the Boy Scouts for credibility, the current situation is particularly risky for both groups. In Boston, Philadelphia, Piedmont near San Francisco, New York City, and in several other cities, Scout councils have made moves with varying degrees of success and publicity, toward allowing homosexuals into their ranks as a direct or indirect consequence of their dependence on the United Way. There seems to be no choice but to appease the custodians of United

Way's prohomosexual antidiscrimination codes when the Scouts rely heavily on United Way for money.

Likewise, the United Way recognizes local decisions to sever funding to the BSA could have consequences for its national reputation. Thousands of once-loyal donors have stopped giving to the United Way in the past few years, particularly in areas where the United Way has ended ties to the Scouts. When the United Way of Forsyth County, North Carolina, announced it was cutting off $429,000 to the Scouts in the aftermath of the *Dale* decision, Winston-Salem Alderman Vernon Robinson drafted and secured passage of a resolution prohibiting the United Way from city premises.[19] A former board member of the Ventura County United Way in California, Dennis Weinberg, announced in 2002 that his private foundation would stop giving to the United Way for "not being truthful about what its agenda is" in dumping the Boy Scouts.[20] Frequently, I receive e-mails from people around America who say they've made the decision to stop giving to the United Way and instead donate to the Scouts.

IN MAJOR CITIES, the United Way now realizes the decision to keep the Scouts or cut them off will be controversial either way. Whichever side pushes the United Way harder, pro-Scout or anti-Scout, usually wins.

The United Way recently formulated a more effective strategy for fending off controversy in cases where the anti-Scouts have won the day. In 2003, two Boy Scout councils—the Capitol Area Council of Texas and the Chicago Area Council—made ominously similar announcements with their local United Ways that the two organizations would be working together in a limited capacity or not at all.[21]

Two things were out of the ordinary. First, partings of the way seemed unnaturally warm. In glowingly positive terms, local Scouting and United Way executives in both Chicago and Austin, Texas, spoke of an "amicable separation." Second, United Way leaders seemed to justify their severance of funding to the Scouts on the basis of factors besides the conflict over nondiscrimination codes.

In Chicago, Illinois, Family Institute President Peter LaBarbera uncovered a hidden agenda behind the Chicago United Way's decision to cut off the Boy Scouts. While the United Way said the cut—from $134,000 to just $25,000—had nothing to do with the Boy Scouts' membership policies, LaBarbera discovered after meeting with executives of both the Scouts and the United Way, that in fact it did. A radical homosexual group called the Chicago Anti-Bashing Network had been lobbying the United Way to cut off the Scouts for years. And nothing other than a blatant bias against the Scouts could have explained the United Way's action; the United Way said the Scouts had failed to correctly complete an application for funding when actually the United Way had changed the application criteria in the midst of the process. Scouting executives explained to LaBarbera that despite their "amicable" outward attitude, they were severely hurt by the slashing of finances.[22]

So why the positive spin on potentially disastrous funding cuts for the Scouts? Because United Way national president Brian Gallagher won't have it any other way. He realizes, correctly of course, that negative portrayal of anti-Scout United Way chapters by supporters of the Boy Scouts will have potential financial consequences for the United Way. He is protecting his organization as any good president or CEO should do by providing talking points for local United Ways that sever ties to Scouting.

The problem is Gallagher isn't supposed to be calling the shots for local United Ways. The United Way claims on nearly every piece of literature, Internet content, and letterhead that its fourteen hundred chapters are "independent" and "separately incorporated," that it does not "dictate policy or funding decisions to local United Ways." But recent developments suggest the United Way may be deceiving its supporters.[23]

Internal United Way correspondence was leaked to the public after Robert Carleson, founder of the Scouting Legal Defense Fund (SLDF) and a former Reagan administration official, contacted local United Ways, seeking accurate information about their relationships with the Boy Scouts. Immediately, Gallagher assumed the defensive. Instead of allowing local United Way chapters to clarify their positions with SLDF, Gallagher forbade locals from replying to Carleson's request letters.

On August 1, 2002, one of Gallagher's assistants, Cynthia Round, executive in charge of brand strategy and marketing, faxed a memo to all United Way professional and volunteer staff across the country.

> We are aware that some local United Ways across the country are receiving correspondence from an organization called Scouting Legal Defense Fund. The stated mission of this organization is to defend and promote scouting. The correspondence specifically requests that the local United Way verifies its funding position regarding local Boy Scout organizations. . . .
>
> Our initial strategy to deal with this organization is to urge the national office of the Boy Scouts of America to communicate directly with Scouting Legal Defense Fund on behalf of United Way. . . .
>
> This attempt to identify United Ways and their positions on funding local Boy Scout organizations is not in BSA's best interest.
>
> UWA will not cooperate with this organization's effort to collect data regarding local United Way allocations. Local United Ways should not comply with this organization's request for information.[24]

There is something strange about that memo. After all, it was unusual for the national United Way to take such a hard stance on simple local data requests. According to its publicly stated structural setup, the national United Way does not dictate policy to local United Ways. And the memo read like a policy paper. But even more questionable than the internal procedures of United Way is its assumption with absolute certainty that it can speak on behalf of the Boy Scouts of America.

After all, why were attempts to identity United Ways and their positions not in the BSA's best interest? Rather than explaining the position, it is simply assumed.

It is a fact, according to the memo, that there is a national United Way "strategy" to "deal with" issues involving the Boy Scouts. In a letter to Robert Carleson, Gallagher wrote:

Dear Mr. Carleson:

I am writing to express my concern about your campaign to identify United Way organizations that may
have reduced or stopped funding to the Boy Scouts and
to request that you discontinue any efforts in this regard. Labeling or characterizing United Way funding
decisions as discriminatory or attributable to the Boy
Scouts' position on sexual orientation is misleading and
raises legal issues that create potential liability for your
organization. . . .

The characterization of local United Way funding decisions as discriminatory is legally inaccurate and may
be libelous. . . .

There is no question that your proposed campaign
will have the opposite effect that you intend with reduced funding for all agencies, including local Boy Scout
councils. Organizational relationships will also suffer as
a result. . . .

The Boy Scouts' policy on sexual orientation has
created challenges in reconciling these two competing
interests. . . .

In the event that you publish any misrepresentations
about United Way organizations, we will not hesitate to
take action to protect the interests of our members.[25]

Carleson had written to the United Ways to clarify his information about specific United Way–Boy Scout relationships and
thereby avoid "misrepresentations." Despite the fact that Carleson
was seeking to maintain accuracy in dealing with local United
Way chapters, Gallagher threatened to take action to protect the
interests of their members if SLDF published "misrepresentations"
about local United Ways.

Interestingly, Gallagher took offense to Carleson's claim that
United Way chapters are discriminating against the Boy Scouts.

In fact, chapters that choose to cut off funds to the Scouts, even if not expressly for the sake of the irreconcilable nondiscrimination codes, do discriminate against the Boy Scouts. The Boy Scouts don't dispute that they discriminate against homosexuals in positions of leadership. And neither the Boy Scouts nor the United Way challenge the legality of their respective choices to discriminate.

Also, Gallagher did not clarify exactly what he meant when he said that asking questions about specific Boy Scout–United Way relationships will hurt the Scouts.

One might believe that relations between the United Way and the Boy Scouts remain naturally cordial, that the reason United Way can speak on behalf of Boy Scouts of America is that the two national organizations remain on good terms. But thinking through the nature of recent Boy Scout–United Way separations, one wonders if the "amicability" is a façade for power-hungry executives in the United Way.

This is precisely why the Boy Scouts' dependency on the United Way is so precarious.

Brian Gallagher contacted Roy Williams, chief executive of the Boy Scouts of America, the result of which was a letter to Robert Carleson warning that his information search was "the opposite of what you intend. In these areas, the United Way's fund raising is being negatively affected, and results in fewer funds for the Boy Scouts and other worthwhile agencies."[26] Williams was apparently afraid for the BSA or anyone else to fight the United Way for its disloyalty to Scouting, fearing that such a fight would harm relationships not only between local councils but with the national organization as well. As the Boy Scouts retain their dependency on the United Way at the same time the United Way rejects the values of Scouting, United Way has the potential to exert influence on the Boy Scouts—as it did in SLDF's case—that could result in perilous moral compromises for the BSA.

In his reply to Williams, Carleson warned of "discrimination against the Scouts by local and possibly the headquarters of the United Way." According to Carleson, "Their memo to their locals and their 'initial strategy' to put pressure on you demonstrates to us that United Way headquarters is part of the problem. Locals are using various tricks to hide their discrimination including requirements for applications that the Scouts cannot meet [as in the Chicago case where Peter LaBarbera discovered application issues attached to anti-Scout bias]. We have information that the national United Way office has been consulted by some locals about how to phrase their doctrine relating to sexual orientation. I believe that the national office of United Way has been cooperating with the anti-Scout locals. Why else would they tell them not to respond to our request for verification?"[27]

Whether the problem is larger than that identified by Carleson is uncertain. But what is clear is that a growing number of United Way chapters are deciding to sever funds to the Scouts.

IN A FURTHER effort to minimize controversy, many, if not all United Way chapters that have severed allocated Boy Scout funding claim they technically continue to give to Scouting. Such is the case in my own community, where despite the depletion of Boy Scouting-earmarked general funds, United Way donors can continue to give to Scouting through the "donor voice" program. Of course, the real issue is allocated funding, but the United Way will continue to claim with pro-Scout donors that because of the donor voice program it still gives to the Boy Scouts.

In some communities, anti-Scout United Ways claim to continue giving to the BSA's Learning for Life educational program, which does not operate like the traditional Boy Scouts and thus does not have membership standards prohibiting homosexuals or atheists. Learning for Life was founded in 1991 as a way for the Boy Scouts of America to take a more direct role in schools across America. Since it was started, Learning for Life has served more than 10 million students from kindergarten to high school while focusing on nine components of character—respect, responsibility, honesty/trust, caring/fairness, perseverance, self-discipline, courage, citizenship, and living skills.[28]

Though Learning for Life makes a positive difference for boys and girls in many communities, it falls short of the legendary quality, values, and leadership that have been a part of the traditional Boy Scout program for more than ninety years. As opposed to camping and hiking and the strategic development of young men, Learning for Life is open to all students in a classroom setting. Learning for Life is good for America, but we can't forget the real Boy Scouts.

WHAT ARE THE alternatives for donors who want their money to go as far as possible? United Way donors can give to the Scouts through the United Way if they use the donor voice program. But doing so gives credibility to an anti-Scout United Way and further entrenches the hazardous dependency the Scouts have on the United Way.

A contribution will go much further if it is given directly to the Boy Scouts. Donors can look up the Boy Scouts in the phone book and send a check, or they can log on to www.scouting.org.

But financial support is not enough to resolve the United Way problem. Nationwide, concerted action must be taken to ensure the United Way does not destroy the Boy Scouts. Americans have plenty of reason to be increasingly vigilant about the United Way's relationship to Boy Scouting. Consider three points:

1. Many employers automatically allow workers to have portions of their paychecks sent to the United Way. In most situations, employees can choose to opt out or arrange to have their donation sent to the Boy Scouts instead.

2. The United Way is simply a middleman for the dispersion of dollars to a variety of nonprofit community organizations. The United Way's mission is not diminished when a donor drops out.

3. Donors can contribute to any nonprofit organization directly. The benefit of doing this is that each dollar will go further without the administrative deductions the United Way takes out.

Since both the BSA and the United Way are private organizations, neither one can be rightfully subject to government control or the overpowering agenda of an outside group of people.

A private organization has a right to its views. The standard applied to the membership policy of the Boy Scouts must be a universal principle: respect the rights of others to associate and formulate opinions. Regardless of our own respect for opposing views, supporters of Scouting have a duty to the future of the country to find other means of giving money to the Boy Scouts.

This need not be a crisis for the Boy Scouts, but it should prompt a serious change in the attitudes of current United Way contributors who support the mission of the Boy Scouts. When in doubt, the best rule of thumb is to give directly to the Boy Scouts of America.

The United Way is making poor choices in major cities around the country. May it suffer the consequences, and may the Boy Scouts reap new rewards from Americans who believe in character and honor.

OTHER CHARITABLE agencies similar to the United Way have chosen to discriminate against the Boy Scouts of America. In Connecticut, state government employees can take advantage of the Connecticut State Employees' Charitable Campaign to support their favorite nonprofit organizations. The list of nine hundred charitable organizations includes the ACLU, People for the Ethical Treatment of Animals, Public Citizen, Greenpeace, the National Abortion Rights Action League, the Hartford Gay/Lesbian Collective, Parents and Friends of Lesbians and Gays, and the National Organization for Women, many of which have declared all-out war on the Boy Scouts and all of which adhere to beliefs and causes far more extreme than the Boy Scouts'.[29]

But in 2000, administrators of Connecticut's charitable giving campaign decided to drop the Boy Scouts from its list of acceptable nonprofit organizations. The Boy Scouts sued the state of Connecticut, and the case made its way to the Second Circuit Court of Appeals, where, in July 2003, it was decided that the state could justifiably exclude the Boy Scouts from its charity list. In late 2003, the Boy Scouts filed another appeal to the U.S. Supreme Court, which was declined. In refusing to challenge the state of Connecticut's discriminatory "antidiscrimination" policy, the Supreme Court set itself against the autonomy of groups like the American Legion and Campus Crusade for Christ, which filed friend-of-the-court briefs in support of the Scouts in the case.[30]

If the Connecticut State Employees' Campaign for Charitable Giving can deliver funding to the nation's most radical leftist organizations, surely it can do the same for a decent organization like the Boy Scouts of America. But reason and honor seem to be lacking in the halls of government these days.

CHAPTER 10

★★

Separation of Scout and State

In the spring of my freshman year in high school, my Boy Scout sash had been filled with all of the twelve required merit badges for Eagle Scout in addition to more than a dozen elective merit badges. All I had left to complete for the Eagle Scout award was the major leadership service project.

I began by asking my church building custodian for a project idea, but nothing came of it. So I called the city of Puyallup office of community relations. Bruce Uhl, who managed the office, was active in local Scouting programs, and his sons had recently become Eagle Scouts. Uhl sent me a list of several dozen projects that required attention around town.

I reviewed the list, but none of the projects particularly suited my interests. Then, Uhl informed me the Puyallup Police Department needed painting in interior offices. I accepted the project and set to work planning. After scheduling a work date, I called Parker Paint to ask for donations of white paint, drop cloths, brushes, and rollers. In addition to supplies, I had to recruit fellow Scouts to volunteer. I worked to secure donated pizza, soda, and cookies from local vendors.

My Eagle Scout service project was a great example of a public–private partnership. Both the city and I benefited from working together to freshen the paint on the walls of the police department offices. What normally would have cost taxpayers several thousand dollars in labor and materials cost almost nothing but time and displaced police officers. Labor was volunteer and materials were donated. A manager from Parker Paint volunteered to spend several hours at the police department to train Scouts and other volunteers in proper painting techniques.

Instead of allocating a portion of the city budget to pay union workers for painting the offices, the city was able to save considerable money and effort by deciding which projects could be accomplished by nonprofessional volunteers and adding those projects to a list for Eagle Scout candidates. In addition to an admirable initiative of fiscal responsibility, the city government was able to engage the two other sectors of human activity—economic and cultural—to accomplish a goal in the public interest.

From local governments to the federal government, the Boy Scouts have benefited from its positive partnership with legislators, city councils, and school boards.

But critics of the Boy Scouts say government partnerships with the Scouts must end.

EVERY PRESIDENT since Theodore Roosevelt and William Howard Taft openly supported Scouting. Some had been Scouts themselves, including Gerald Ford, who was an Eagle Scout.[1]

But Bill Clinton was different. Clinton was the only president in history to turn down a request to speak at a national Boy Scout Jamboree. In 1993, Clinton refused to attend the Jamboree only seventy miles from the White House, perhaps because the homosexual movement had been a key special interest group behind Clinton's election to the presidency.[2] Several years later, in a 1999 letter to Scouting for All, Vice President Al Gore wrote, "Thank you for all your efforts against discrimination."[3]

Four days before the *Dale* decision, President Clinton called for a reconsideration of the federal government's ties to the Boy Scouts. On June 24, 2000, executive order 13160 left Clinton's desk, banning discrimination in the federal government on the basis of "race, sex, color, national origin, disability, religion, age, sexual orientation, and status as apparent in federally conducted

education and training programs."[4] The executive order meant
nothing less than a full severance of ties between federal government agencies and the Boy Scouts in "education and training programs." During World War II Scouts worked in their communities
to sell war bonds. During the energy crisis of the 1970s, Scouts
volunteered to lead conservation projects.

The agency most affected by the executive order was the U.S.
Department of the Interior. Since the department is in charge of
America's national parks, it had a long and fruitful relationship
with the Boy Scouts. For years, the Scouts have been allowed to
use national parks for Jamborees.

Interior Department diversity officer Nattie Silva conducted a
systematic survey of federal agencies to ensure compliance with
the executive order. Once agencies were reviewed, the order would
have dissolved a number of Boy Scout training activities once provided with federal agencies.[5]

Congressman J. C. Watts of Oklahoma called it "an absolute
insult to families and Scouts."[6]

The memo became an issue in the 2000 presidential campaign. Texas Governor George W. Bush, the Republican presidential nominee, stated, "I am troubled by this memo." He added his
hope that Clinton would not, "allow them [Boy Scouts] to be shut
out of federal lands."[7]

Two months after the executive order was issued, Interior Department solicitor John Leshy submitted Nattie Silva's report to
Attorney General Janet Reno. Leshy asked the attorney general,
specifically, whether the BSA could continue to use federal property for its summer Jamborees under the new executive order.[8]

According to Robert Knight of the Culture and Family Institute, "Ignoring the rule of law, the Clinton administration appears
to be readying a shocking attack on the Boy Scouts; Americans
need to fight back by telling the administration and the homosexual groups that are prompting such attacks: Keep your hands
off the Boy Scouts."[9] The American people did fight back against
the president. Citizens wrote letters and e-mails, called, and demonstrated. Under intense public pressure, Reno responded that the

BSA could continue to use federal lands.[10] Given the broad public support for Scouting, the Clinton administration's attempts to sever government ties to Scouting failed.

The Boy Scouts have had a better experience working with President George W. Bush. In July 31, 2001, Bush spoke to the Boy Scout Jamboree.[11] Bush's videotaped remarks were shown to thirty-two thousand Boy Scouts gathered at Fort A. P. Hill in Virginia. He had planned to speak the previous evening, but rain caused him to cancel his actual appearance. His words reflected a refreshing measure of support. "Every society depends on trust and loyalty, on courtesy and kindness, on bravery and reverence," Bush said. "Times and challenges change, but the values of Scouting will never change. What you have learned in Scouting will see you through life. In good times and difficult ones, the Scout Motto will always help you 'Be prepared.' And whatever you do, the Scout Oath will always guide you—'On your honor' do your best."[12]

FOLLOWING THE Dale decision, ultraleftist Congresswoman Lynn Woolsey decided to wage all-out political jihad on the Boy Scouts of America. First, the California Democrat drafted a letter to President Clinton, asking that he resign as honorary president of the Boy Scouts of America.[13] The first honorary president of the BSA was William Howard Taft in 1911.[14]

Signing Woolsey's letter were Congress members (all Democrats) Bob Filner, Barbara Lee, George Miller, and Nancy Pelosi of California; Cynthia McKinney of Georgia; Tammy Baldwin of Wisconsin; Barney Frank and John Oliver of Massachusetts; Janice Schakowsky of Illinois; and Jerold Nadler of New York.[15]

Each of the anti-Scout members of Congress who signed the letter to President Clinton held membership in the U.S. House Progressive Caucus, a wing of the Democratic Socialists of America. DSA identifies its primary objective as "building progressive movements for social change while establishing an openly socialist presence in American communities and politics."[16] Instead of a veiled conspiracy to implement socialism through American government, the members of the House Progressive Caucus were unabashed, outspoken socialists. Private initiative and free institutions that endorse moral character were, according to Woolsey and the House Progressive Caucus, unworthy of presidential acknowledgement.

Woolsey's second shot at the Scouts was a bill reading: "To repeal the Federal charter of the Boy Scouts of America."[17]

Congress first approved a national charter—an honorary status stating that Congress supports the patriotic, educational, or scientific goals of an organization and that the organization that holds the charter is guaranteed rights to its name in perpetuity—for the Boy Scouts of America in 1916.

Other organizations with discriminatory membership standards have unquestioned congressional charters. It is the policy of one charter holder, the Catholic War Veterans, that "an applicant shall be a member of the Catholic Church" in addition to having served in the armed forces.[18] Another chartered group, the Jewish War Veterans, requires its members to be Jewish.[19] And the Veterans of Foreign Wars includes only veterans who participated in military campaigns and battles. "The fundamental difference between our Organization and other veteran organizations, and one in which we take great pride, is our eligibility qualifications," says the VFW eligibility requirements.[20]

Though I am neither a Catholic nor a Jew, I do not take offense to the Catholic War Veterans and Jewish War Veterans each holding a congressional charter. I am glad those organizations have a charter, for their members have made it possible for America to remain free. And the Boy Scouts serve America's communities and make it possible for generations of young men to understand more fully the patriotic duties inherent in being an American. The Scouts, too, are fully deserving of a congressional charter.

Unsatisfied with the Supreme Court's decision to allow private organizations to hold autonomy over their own membership standards for private organizations, Woolsey thought Congress was obligated to destroy the Boy Scouts instead. "If both the Court and Congress convey the message that discrimination is okay, I fear we encourage other organizations to discriminate as well."[21] Ironically, Woolsey's own job as a member of Congress was contingent on a series of constitutional qualifications and the discrimination of her voting constituents. To serve in Congress, a person must be a citizen of at least twenty-five years of age.

On the floor of Congress, Woolsey asserted, "For me and the bill's supporters, this is not a question of whether the Boy Scouts have a right to establish anti-gay policy. It is a question of whether the Boy Scouts' anti-gay policy is right."[22] This from a woman whose political persuasion is known for its intolerance of "legislating morality." Because legislating morality in its most coercive form is exactly what Woolsey, a public official, proposed on behalf of a private organization.

Disgusted by Woolsey's twisted illogic about "tolerance," Congressman Steve Buyer took the floor of Congress: "This bill promotes intolerance. The Boy Scouts respect other people's right to hold differing opinions than their own and ask others to respect their belief. Extremist Democrats believe just the opposite. They believe that if one does not subscribe to their beliefs and their view of the world, then one is intolerant and must be chastised. Tolerance does not require a moral equivalency. Rather, it implies a willingness to recognize and respect the beliefs of others. The Boy Scouts are a model of inclusiveness."[23] Only twelve members of the House voted to approve the measure. A total of 362 cast an honorable no vote.[24] Congressional leaders had recently organized the Congressional Scouting Caucus, a bipartisan group of about eighty representatives who were Eagle Scouts.[25] The Congressional Scouting Caucus scored a victory over the House Progressive Caucus.

But when it came time for the U.S. Senate to stand behind the Boy Scouts, the vote count was much closer. Former South Carolina Senator Jesse Helms proposed an amendment to the Better Education for Students and Teachers Act mandating that school districts prohibit discrimination against the Boy Scouts in order to obtain federal funding. The Office of Civil Rights in the U.S. Department of Education would be authorized by the Helms amendment to investigate school districts that discriminate; the

Department of Education would sever federal funding if the district failed to allow equal access.

Helms was addressing a serious problem that threatened to grow following the 2000 National Education Association Convention at which delegates had passed a resolution urging "state and local affiliates to work with school boards to establish policies requiring that all private organizations using school facilities have nondiscriminatory membership policies."[26] Though the NEA resolution didn't mention "Boy Scouts," the NEA had taken a stance far from its position ninety years earlier when it declared the Boy Scouts a solution to youth social problems like boredom, substance abuse, and gang activity.[27] In introducing the amendment, Helms explained: "Radical militants . . . are pressuring school districts across the country to exclude the Boy Scouts of America from federally funded public school facilities based on what they did in one instance. They decided to press for exclusion of the Boy Scouts from the schools because the Boy Scouts would not agree to surrender their first amendment rights and because they would not accept the agenda of the radical left."[28]

Washington Senator Patty Murray objected, "The Helms amendment addresses a problem that does not exist. Groups like the Scouts already have equal access through existing law."[29] Actually, when the Helms amendment was offered, June 14, 2001, nine of the nation's largest school districts had denied access to the Boy Scouts.

New Hampshire Senator Bob Smith responded to the sentiments of liberal Democrats who criticized the Boy Scouts. Smith's speech was rebroadcast on radio and television programs around the nation:

> These are the boys we want to keep from having their meetings in schools that receive billions of taxpayer dollars. I never thought I would see the day when I would have to stand on the Senate floor and go to bat for the Boy Scouts to have that right. . . .
>
> The largest voluntary youth organization and movement in the world—the Boy Scouts—is under siege right on the Senate floor. Six million American boys are mem-

bers from a wide diversity—religious, ethnic, economic, disability, special needs, honor students, Eagle Scouts, all of it—are under siege. . . .

This tradition should be revered and protected by the Federal Government, not attacked by the Federal Government. We shouldn't discriminate against an organization because it teaches boys morality. . . .

They ought to be held in esteem. When they ask to have a meeting, they ought to be asked: Which room do you want? What have they done that is so wrong? The answer is, nothing. What they have done is so right. And they are being punished for it.[30]

When the votes were counted, some Democrats said yes, including John Breaux of Louisiana, Robert Byrd of West Virginia, Fritz Hollings of South Carolina, Timothy Johnson of South Dakota, and Zell Miller of Georgia. Three Republicans said no—Lincoln Chafee of Rhode Island, Arlen Specter of Pennsylvania, and George Voinovich of Ohio.[31] In the end, the vote could not have been closer, unless Vice President Dick Cheney had been called to break a tie. The vote was 51–49. The Helms amendment passed, barely.

The U.S. House of Representatives was called on again to defend the Scouts shortly after September 11, 2001. Under jurisdiction of Article I: Section 8 of the U.S. Constitution—"Congress shall have the power to exercise exclusive legislation in all cases whatsoever over the District [capitol]"—Indiana Republican Congressman John Hostettler proposed an amendment to reverse a decision by the Washington, D.C., Human Rights Commission forcing the local Boy Scouts to admit two homosexual Scoutmasters.[32] Congress voted 262–152 in favor of the amendment.[33]

Essentially, the Human Rights Commission had used the coercive authority of government to force the Boy Scouts, a private organization, to accept members who violated its core principles. While the congressional jurisdiction over the District of Columbia allowed Congress to reverse the D.C. Human Rights Commission, other major cities and local governments are increasingly aggressive in their efforts to condemn the Boy Scouts.

WHEN I WAS in elementary school, the local Cub Scout pack would send an occasional pile of recruitment literature to my teacher for distribution. The brochure would make it home to my parents with a stack of graded spelling quizzes and weekly progress reports. I didn't actually join the Scouts until I was older, but many of my friends signed up to be Cub Scouts as a result of the literature they took home.

In 1991, the Oakland and San Francisco school boards passed resolutions banning the Boy Scouts from recruiting students in school buildings during school hours.[34] More recently, California's Davis School Board banned the Scouts from using school newsletters or bulletin boards to recruit students.[35]

In 1996, Portland Cub Scout parents went to a local first-grade classroom to hand out wristbands reading, "Come Join Cub Scout Pack 16! Round-Up for New Cub Scouts for Boys in Grades 1-5." Six-year-old Remington Powell went home excited to join the Cub Scouts with his friends. But his mother, atheist Nancy Powell, told him he could not join because he was forbidden to believe in God. Ms. Powell spent the next two years harassing school district administrators at every level to get them to adopt a policy similar to those in Oakland and San Francisco.[36]

In 1998, she asked the ACLU to file a lawsuit against the Portland schools, alleging discrimination against her son. On the Tom Leykis radio talk show, she fumed, "I, personally, am on a campaign—again, personally on a campaign to avoid the Boy Scouts in every possible way. . . . The Boy Scouts of America don't belong in public schools. They are a religious organization, and we have separation of church and state."[37]

After a court told the Portland schools that Scouts could continue to recruit in classrooms, Powell and the ACLU went to the Oregon Court of Appeals where it was decided in March 2005 that Portland had unfairly discriminated against atheists. As of this writing, the Portland Schools are leaning toward an official policy excluding the Boy Scouts from recruiting in classrooms.[38]

Other school districts have acted against the Boy Scouts with less conflict.

In September 2000, New York Community School Board 2 voted to ban Scouts from the special use of school property. The District 2 directive prohibited schools from sponsoring troops and banned BSA recruitment on campuses.[39]

Shortly thereafter, New York Community School Board 15 became the second in the New York public school system to prevent the BSA from using its facilities or recruiting its students. The school board resolution stated: "Community School Board 15 is dismayed that one of the nation's most revered civic institutions . . . would proclaim itself to be a discriminatory group. . . . Gay youth, who are often targets of anti-gay harassment and brutality, need and deserve BSA programs and support. . . . Official sponsorship of BSA activities—especially public school sponsorship—may send a message to both gay youth and non-gay youth that discrimination based on sexual orientation is acceptable."[40] Decisions by New York community school boards to exclude the Boy Scouts gave rise to a wave of similar decisions in major school districts, cities, and counties across the country.

In Florida, the Broward County School Board, presiding over one of the largest school districts in the country, voted in November 2000 to discontinue a facility use agreement with the South Florida Council of the Boy Scouts of America. As the basis for terminating the agreement, the school board cited its nondiscrimination policy, one that prohibits "the rental use or enjoyment of school facilities or services by any group or organization which discriminates on the basis of age, race, color, disability, gender, marital status, national origin, religion or sexual orientation."[41] Because of the policy's language, the Scouts weren't even allowed to pay rent to use schools. As a result, fifty-seven Cub Scout and Boy Scout units were without meeting facilities.

The South Florida Council filed a lawsuit in U.S. District Court, arguing that the district rented its facilities to evening basketball programs that discriminate on age, groups like the Girl Scouts that discriminate on sex, and church groups that discriminate on religious belief. The school district argued that the

Boy Scouts could incur emotional damage by continuing their presence in Broward schools.[42]

After hearing the arguments in *Boy Scouts of America v. Till*, U.S. District Court Judge Donald Middlebrooks decided in favor of the South Florida Council. In his preliminary injunction against the Broward County School Board, Judge Middlebrooks stated, "The government must abstain from regulating speech when the specific motivating ideology or the opinion or perspective of the speaker is the rationale for the restrictions." The judge further noted that a school district may decide to adopt a "nondiscrimination policy" for itself but must allow equal access to its facilities.[43]

On October 8, 2000, the Gay, Lesbian, and Straight Education Network held a summit in Chicago to rally education leaders against the Boy Scouts. GLSEN presented a prestigious Pathfinder Award to Dr. Carol Johnson, the superintendent of Minneapolis public schools, for her work on behalf of homosexuals.[44] In her acceptance remarks, Johnson announced that her school district would prohibit schools from chartering troops. Nine hundred Minneapolis-area Scouts in twenty-five troops were faced with finding new meeting places.[45]

According to the *Boston Globe* in September 2003, approximately 350 school districts in ten states around the country have ended sponsorship of or providing facilities for the Boy Scouts of America.[46]

CITIES AND COUNTIES have been equally intolerant in their treatment of the Boy Scouts.

In 2003—three-quarters of a century after the Philadelphia City Council voted in favor of allowing the Philadelphia Cradle of Liberty Boy Scout Council to use a half acre of public land at 22nd and Winter streets "in perpetuity" for its headquarters—the Scout council was told that it could no longer occupy the headquarters building. The Scouts' exclusion of homosexuals conflicted with the city's nondiscrimination code. As discussed in chapter 1, the Scouts had one year to leave the land or compromise on moral virtue and retain use of the headquarters.

Malcolm Lazin, executive director of the Philadelphia-based homosexual group Equality Forum, told the *Philadelphia Inquirer* that "the city is now obliged to terminate the lease. This is an organization that discriminates and should not be given what is, in essence, a sweetheart deal." And Stacey Sobel of the Center for Lesbian and Gay Civil Rights said, "This is another message to the local and national Boy Scouts that they cannot continue to do business as usual."[47]

Nondiscrimination codes like Philadelphia's—which includes immoral behavior like homosexuality as a protected category—have exacted a great cost from the civic virtue of our cities. No one should be forced to be trustworthy, loyal, helpful, friendly, courteous, kind, obedient, cheerful, thrifty, brave, clean, and reverent. But the city of Philadelphia should have the instinctive desire to say it encourages and endorses those things. America should never have come so near to dismantling the statue of a Boy Scout in front of the Philadelphia BSA headquarters instead of exalting it high on the pedestal of civic and community respectability.

Since government is a reflection of the people and exists to serve the people, government cannot afford neutrality on issues of moral permanence. Government itself is not the moral compass of society, but it cannot rightly exist without moral guidance. The government cannot declare itself stuck in the middle of a road between right and wrong when the war between the two will destroy it in the center of the battle. George Will wrote, "A society that dedicates itself to the pursuit of happiness had better dedicate itself, including its government, to the pursuit of the virtues indispensable to ordered liberty."[48]

Governing bodies at the federal, state, and local levels should, as they have, acknowledge and support the principles of virtue and honor identified in the Scout oath and law. For the Boy Scouts exist, to paraphrase the "Battle Hymn of the Republic," to make boys righteous and so to make men free. And a small Boy Scout troop works much better on the hearts of young men than a thousand legions of government bureaucrats, educrats, and legislators trying to improve society.

The twelve virtues listed in the Scout law are far more powerful—and more liberating—than the laws and statutes a congress,
legislature, or city council can create. The force of self-control is
most important in regulating a free people. Freedom is not, as
has been supposed by the cultural Left of the past forty years,
the ability to do whatever one chooses to do. Freedom is only
possible in a nation that values high and uncompromising moral
character.

"The foundation of our national policy," said George Washington in his first inaugural address, "must be laid in the pure
and immutable principles of private morality."[49] Indeed, the most
important ally of sound public policy is solid private character. "In
America," wrote William J. Bennett, "general liberty cannot survive a dearth of virtue, and public policy cannot succeed without
addressing the issue of values directly."[50]

Why are values important for government? Because the people
affected by government policies have souls. As Chief Scout Citizen Theodore Roosevelt said, "The most perfect machinery of government will not keep us as a nation if there is not within us a
soul."[51]

IN RECENT YEARS, a new war is being waged against the soul
in city halls and Congress, in courts, and on school boards. In one
battle of this war, government officials at all levels have worked on
behalf of their more left-leaning constituents to separate the Boy
Scouts entirely from the cooperative strains of public policy. This
movement is symbolic of a growing rift between government and
private morality that Washington said was the very foundation of
public policy.

Government no longer sees itself as a reflection of the people
and as a repository of honorable men. Instead, government promotes radical egalitarianism and radical individualism by catering
to the interests of those who claim minority status—in this case,
homosexuals and atheists. Thus, government systematically lifts
the responsibility for morality from the great institutions of society
and trumps that responsibility with the newly minted rights of in-

dividuals not merely to make whatever moral choice they choose, but to have their choices officially sanctioned and protected by the force of government.

But the Boy Scouts are not a protected minority, and their loudest critics are.

"Elite culture now sees the highest function of government as correcting the petty prejudices of the citizens, even if that means destroying civil society in the process," said Heather MacDonald. "If government's crusade against so-called bigotry means eviscerating the Scouts, it is long past time to shut the crusade down."[52]

Government ought to have an interest in equality, but if that interest goes so far as to render it morally neutral, as we now witness, politicians and bureaucrats no longer have to swear "on my honor" before entering into an agreement, raising taxes, creating a new program, proclaiming a new right, or usurping a new responsibility that rightly belongs to the people.

The result, Peter Kreeft wrote, is that "moral values have become both privatized and collectivized."[53] Morality is privatized in that most government bodies no longer consider virtue to be any of their business. Morality is collectivized in that most government bodies have begun to enforce with passion that surrogate morality known as political correctness.

A government without morals is a government out of touch with the higher law—"the Laws of Nature and of Nature's God" spoken of by the Founding Fathers in the Declaration of Independence. And when government is faced with the task of creating laws while lacking a standard other than equality on which to do so, both law and the character of the people necessary to comply with law go by the wayside.

Thus, when it comes to preserving constitutional government, the character of the people is an absolute necessity. History shows that laws and government authority are applied as coercion when the people cease to control their own passions. When, by deficit of the people's virtue, the authority of government must be applied to gain control of the people, the force is always less efficient and the people are always less free.

America was founded to be morally straight so it could be politically free. "We have no government armed with power capable
of contending with human passions unbridled by morality and religion," wrote John Adams. "Our constitution was made only for
a moral and religious people. It is wholly inadequate for a government of any other."[54]

CALIFORNIA ASSEMBLYWOMAN Jackie Goldberg (D-Los
Angeles) is one of the elites who would say that the morality
and religion spoken of by John Adams are better termed "discrimination." Goldberg has been a militant feminist lesbian since
she spent the sixties as a radical peacenik at the University of
California–Berkeley. Goldberg recently sponsored bills to rid
California's schools of American Indian mascots and to extend
spousal employment benefits to partners of homosexual employees. And in Assembly Resolution 89 in April 2003, Goldberg
wrote, "The discriminatory policy of the Boy Scouts of America
is contrary to the policy of the State of California."[55]

Goldberg believed that the state of California had a compelling
interest to be involved in destroying the Boy Scouts. "The policy
of the Boy Scouts to bar from membership or leadership qualified individuals based solely on the basis of their sexual orientation or religious belief causes harm to the innumerable boys and
men . . . who, regardless of their hard work and merits, are denied
the opportunity to . . . participate in any way in the Boy Scouts of
America."[56] The resolution also included a glorious commendation
of Scouting for All.

The California Assembly passed Resolution 89 by a vote of
43–2. An additional thirty-six assembly members were listed in
that roll call as "absent, abstaining, or not voting." A few months
later, the California State Senate passed Resolution 89 by a vote of
22–15.[57]

The vitriolic odium of Goldberg and the majority of her col-
leagues is terrifying. If the California legislature has the authority to advise the Boy Scouts on its morality, it can do the same
for churches and other private organizations that believe in virtue

and decency. Goldberg told the *Roseville Press-Tribune,* "I think it's important for the State of California to speak up and not be silent, and to say to the Scouts, if you have a religious belief, that's your belief. But keep it separate from a youth-serving agency that serves kids in all neighborhoods."[58]

In other words, Scouting is OK, as long as it doesn't stand for anything.

CHAPTER 11

★★★

Duty to God

Troop 174 has a tradition of holding an informal "church" service when Scouting adventures fall on a Sunday. They're held in what Baden-Powell called "the church of the outdoors," and they tend to be an occasion to reflect on God's creation.

Among my most memorable experiences as a Scout was a church service I led on a late Sunday afternoon one July while my troop was traveling through the Dinosaur National Monument area of Utah and Colorado. We drove up a narrow, steep road until we came to the dead-end at the summit. There we were afforded a glimpse of the canyon below from the majestic Plug Hat Butte as the sun was declining in the cloudless sky, projecting a golden touch on the tranquil valleys below. Stepping out to a small rocky ledge, we seemed for a moment to be held in the gentle hands of a mighty, loving God. While eleven Boy Scouts stood in stunned silence at the awe-inspiring beauty, His peace radiated around us.

Before the short walk from the troop van to the overlook, I had retrieved my tattered white camping Bible. As I recall, I chose to read Psalm 8 for church on that Sunday afternoon: "Lord, our Lord, how magnificent is Your name throughout the earth! You have covered the heavens with Your majesty. . . . what is man that You remember him? . . . You made him lord over the works of Your hands; You put everything under his feet" (vv. 1, 4a, 6).

After I said a few words about my thoughts on this ancient psalm of David, the wonders of creation, and the blessings of life, I opened the floor for a time of prayer. Most Scouts chimed in with a few words of thanksgiving and invocation of God's blessings for the road ahead. I closed the prayer and we reloaded the van and drove into the setting sun.

UNLIKE SO MANY organizations whose habits of invoking God to open a meeting are a thing of the past, the Boy Scouts have left the great oath unabridged in respect toward God. It follows that "a Scout is reverent." If not, he isn't really a Scout.

According to the Boy Scout handbook's description of the twelfth point in the Scout law:

A Scout is reverent toward God. He is faithful in his religious duties. He respects the beliefs of others.

Wonders all around us remind us of our faith in God. We find it in the secrets of creation and in the great mysteries of the universe. It exists in the kindness of people and in the teachings of our families and religious leaders. We show our reverence by living our lives according to the ideals of our beliefs.

Throughout your life you will encounter people expressing their reverence in many different ways. The Constitution of the United States guarantees each of us the freedom to believe and worship as we wish without government interference. It is your duty to respect and defend others' rights to their religious beliefs even when they are different from your own.[1]

Though their program largely reflects a Christian ethic, the Boy Scouts is not a strictly Christian organization as many critics have alleged.

Scouting simply professes it is impossible to be physically strong, mentally awake, and morally straight without striving to fulfill a duty to a divine power higher than mere self-interest. The Boy Scouts of America adopted their current declaration of religious principle in 1970. Reaffirmed in 1991, it states, "The Boy Scouts of America has always been committed to the moral, ethical, and spiritual development of our youth. Scouting is not a religion, but duty to God is a basic tenet of the Scout Oath and Law."[2] Of course, specific religious direction is not and never has been the function of the Boy Scouts of America, but a personal religious faith is the paramount obligation of an individual Scout. Without recognizing God, it is impossible to obey the rest of the Scout law.

Critics of Scouting imagine it is possible to exhibit character without professing a personal faith in God. But character is not only what feels good or what has a positive impact on the feelings of others. In fact, character is not even the oft-quoted "what you're doing when nobody else is looking." Character is how we act in the presence of Almighty God. And as far as we know, it is impossible to escape the watch of God.

Character and faith are indelibly connected, a fact realized by relativists and absolutists, atheists and Christians alike. Columnist Bill Murchison wrote, "There is such a thing as morality because there is such a thing as religion. Absent a Creator God, moral codes reduce to constantly shifting ethical preferences."[3] Writer Peter Kreeft quoted three authors: The Russian novelist Fyodor Dostoyevsky declared, "If God does not exist, everything is permissible." Sartre wrote, "All possibility of finding values in a heaven of ideas disappears along with Him. There can be no a priori Good since there is no infinite and perfect consciousness to think it." And G. K. Chesterton observed, "If I did not believe in God, I should still want my doctor, my lawyer, and my banker to do so."[4]

The most pronounced feature of the current relativist age is its rejection of God and all things spiritual. In the late 1800s, a syphilis-plagued philosopher named Friedrich Nietzsche proclaimed, "God is dead."[5] Coupled with that blatant atheism was Nietzsche's philosophy on truth: "This is the final truth, that there is no truth!"[6] Six and a half decades after the death of Nietzsche, the cover of *Time* magazine revealed a shocking indicator about the state of American culture. It read, "God is dead."

In 1962, the U.S. Supreme Court decided that public schools violated the First Amendment if students or teachers led any type of prayer. The God-is-dead mentality began to creep into the establishment of America's legal and educational communities. Popular culture began to sing, write, photograph, draw, and speak it.

The Supreme Court continued to use the First Amendment in promoting an atheist agenda in public schools. In 1974, it banned the use of the Ten Commandments in public schools. Six years later, the Bible was censored from classrooms. By 2000, the Supreme Court had even banned prayer at school sports and graduation events.

When young Americans of the past thirty years have looked at "In God We Trust" emblazoned on the coins in their pocket, or have recited "one nation under God" in the pledge of allegiance, or have read that our rights come from the Creator in the Declaration of Independence, there have been conflicting messages. Is God important for America, or is God to be left out of the public square?

WHEN I VISITED Philmont Scout Ranch in 2001 with ten fellow Scouts and two adult leaders, my peers elected me chaplain aide for the two-week journey through New Mexico's Sangre de Cristo Mountains.

We arrived at Philmont base camp in Cimarron on a balmy Friday afternoon, and after a series of routine check-ins and medical clearances, I was instructed to report to the chaplain aide's orientation. In the late afternoon, I headed to the meeting on a sprawling green lawn outside a row of Spanish mission-style buildings. The Protestant chaplain was giving the orientation that day, and he introduced himself as a pastor from Ohio who spent his summers ministering at Philmont. It seemed like an enjoyable job, or at least the chaplain was enjoying himself.

The chaplain gave each aide a pamphlet of daily devotional exercises titled *Eagles Soaring High: Religious Worship for Christians, Muslims, and Jews.* The pamphlet featured the writings of nine religious leaders from different walks of faith and included a nondenominational section as well. The chaplain also noted that small green, lightweight New Testaments (published by the United Methodist Scouting Association) were on hand for any Scout who wanted one.

Before departing on the trail, our troop guide, a twenty-year-old college student from Albuquerque, gave us small identification tags on which we were to write our names. The tag was also printed with useful camping and outdoor information and the Philmont grace, which is a generic prayer. But it was simple, memorizable, and meaningful: "For food, for raiment, for life, for opportunity, for friendship and fellowship, we thank thee, O Lord. Amen."

The grace is said before meals both on the trail and at base camp.

During the course of our weeks at Philmont, I led Troop 174 in devotions each night. Since there were no Muslims and Jews in our troop, we naturally went with Christian devotions, which suited everyone, even those among us who were less devout in religious practice. After a Scripture reading, we would reflect on the day just past with a Boy Scout ritual called "thorns and roses." This was an opportunity for each Scout to give an honest appraisal of one or two things he liked the most about the day and what he most disliked.

On our return from the trail, Troop 174 attended chapel services led by the Philmont chaplains. Daily services were offered in the Protestant, Catholic, Jewish, and Mormon faiths. The services were voluntary, but Scouts were encouraged to attend. And the ministries were supported by offerings, not camp tuition.

Most summer Scout camps offer at the least a nondenominational Christian chapel during the week.

THERE CAN BE no mistaking the religious equality in Scouting. The Boy Scouts of America encourages youth from all faiths to be active participants. The BSA's Religious Relationships Committee oversees the granting of religious patches to Scouts who demonstrate exemplary service to their faith group. Twenty-nine religious groups award patches to Scouts through the Religious Relationships Committee. The list includes Armenians, Baha'i, Baptist, Buddhist, Christian Science, Eastern Catholic, Eastern Orthodox, Episcopal, Hindu, Islamic, Jewish, Lutheran, Maher Baba, Moravian, Mormon, Presbyterian, Quaker, Roman Catholic, United Methodist, and Zoroastrian. Clearly, the Boy Scouts are far from being devoid of religious diversity.[7]

But, make no doubt about it, the Boy Scouts do insist on belief in God. Just because there's religious diversity doesn't mean the false faith of atheism is an accepted religion. The ban on atheists is nothing new for the Scouts. Since BSA was founded, several hundred atheists have been told that they could not serve in positions of Scout leadership.[8]

THERE WASN'T MUCH controversy surrounding decisions to exclude atheists from Scouting until 1985, when fifteen-year-old Paul Trout of Charlottesville, Virginia, admitted to a board of review for his advancement to Life Rank that he did not believe in God. The national BSA expelled Trout since he apparently rejected God. Then, after the ACLU had threatened a lawsuit against the Scouts, Trout changed his profession on a technicality to say he "did not believe in God as a supreme being." The BSA decided it was not its job to define what God is so long as a Scout acknowledges a belief in God. On this technical matter, which may be called a serious compromise on the part of the Boy Scouts, Paul Trout was readmitted to his troop.[9]

Still, the policy banning avowed atheists—those who flatly refused to swear to do their best to do their duty to God—remained in place.

IN 1989, ELLIOT WELSH'S six-year-old son Mark came home from school with a flyer recruiting new Tiger Scouts for a chapter in Hinsdale, Illinois, a suburb of Chicago. When Mr. Welsh discovered that he needed to accompany his son in Tiger Scout activities, he attended a parent meeting with Mark at an elementary school gymnasium. At the meeting, Welsh was asked to sign the Scout declaration of religious principles. As an agnostic, Welsh hated the mention of God, and he tried to teach his son to feel the same way. He refused to sign the document.[10]

Welsh sued the West Suburban Council and its Tiger Scout chapter in March 1990.[11]

The case came before the U.S. Court of Appeals for the Seventh Circuit on November 13, 1992. A decision was made on

May 17, 1993. One of the judges sided with Welsh. The other two sided with the Boy Scouts. Judge John Coffey delivered the majority opinion: "The leadership of many in our government is a testimonial to the success of Boy Scout activities. . . . In recent years, single-parent families, gang activity, the availability of drugs and other factors have increased the dire need for support structures like the Boy Scouts. When the government, in this instance, through the courts, seeks to regulate the membership of an organization like the Boy Scouts in a way that scuttles its founding principles, we run the risk of undermining one of the seedbeds of virtue that cultivates the sorts of citizens our nation so desperately needs." The court ruled that since the Boy Scouts are a private organization, they have the right to determine their membership standards. In addition, Judge Coffey pointed out that in no way was the BSA violating the Civil Rights Act of 1964, because, he reasoned, the BSA is an activity, not a facility or "place of public accommodation."[12]

Interestingly, in 1916, the larger nearby Chicago Board of Education endorsed Scouting as an effective remedy to crime. Members of Congress took the Chicago board resolution as reasoning to enact the BSA national charter.[13]

During the Welsh case in 1993, atheist activist Todd Pence authored a pamphlet in which he argued that the Boy Scouts policy against atheism was flawed: "The situation in the modern BSA is somewhat reminiscent of that in Sir Thomas More's Utopia, in which the citizens of the fictitious country were given the right to choose any religion to practice, with the exception of Atheism, which was punishable by death."[14]

In no way does the BSA advocate a culture of disrespect toward the dignity of those who reject God. It is impossible to compare the BSA to a society that kills its atheists. While atheism is certainly a dangerous belief, its tolerance in a free society results from the worldview advocated in Scouting. In a world of atheism, man is the standard; in that world a belief in God would be punishable by death. Scouting teaches a respect for all people, a tolerance for all faiths.

Attorney James Randall of Anaheim, California, paid close attention to the *Welsh* case. Randall's twin sons, Michael and William, were members of a local Cub Scout pack in 1989 when they were seven years old. Two years after joining the Pack, the Randall twins were working on the completion of religious requirements for a badge when they disclosed they did not believe in God. They refused to complete the requirements.[15]

James Randall had trained his sons well as atheists. James Randall himself represented his sons as an attorney, and in 1991, Randall filed a lawsuit against the Mount Diablo Council (which incidentally was also fighting the lawsuit by homosexual Scoutmaster applicant Timothy Curran).[16]

In June 1992, Orange County Superior Court Judge Richard O. Frazee ruled in favor of the Randall twins on the grounds they could not be excluded by the BSA "because of their beliefs, or lack of them."[17] Since judges in the Curran case had ruled that the Scouts have a constitutionally protected right to discriminate in membership, the Supreme Court accepted the task of deciding between the conflicting Randall and Curran decisions. In both cases, the California court ruled that "under California's 1959 civil rights law, the Scouts are not a business establishment and so are free, as is any private club, to set membership policies as they see fit."[18]

THERE IS NO QUESTION that the Scouts, a private organization, have the constitutionally protected right to practice duty to God and reverence. Yet legitimate questions arise when the Boy Scouts are involved in partnerships with public entities. Does it violate the "separation of church and state" when the Scouts are engaged in public–private partnerships described in the previous chapter?

According to U.S. District Court Judge Napoleon Jones, the Boy Scouts are a religious organization whose eighty-eight-year relationship with the city of San Diego violated the First Amendment when he ruled it must be ended. In August 2003, Jones handed down his ruling as hundreds of Boy Scouts were enjoying summer camp at San Diego's Camp Balboa. Soon, the Boy Scouts will be ejected from their historic sixteen-acre camp and council headquarters building.[19]

With "overwhelming and uncontradicted evidence," Jones found that the Boy Scouts are a religious organization and were given preferential treatment when the city first agreed to let the Boy Scouts use public land in Balboa Park nearly nine decades ago. In 2000, a lesbian couple and an agnostic couple joined with the ACLU to file the lawsuit against the city. They claimed to feel excluded by the Boy Scouts' religious policies in particular.[20] "Belief in God is and always has been central to BSA's principles and purposes," Judge Jones wrote. "Adult leaders are expected to reinforce in Scouts the values of duty to God and reverence."[21]

If there is "overwhelming and uncontradicted evidence" for the presence of God in the life of a Boy Scout, there is evidence of a similar nature for God's role in the public square on Main Street USA. Religious mottoes, preambles, and texts were not an afterthought to the people who wrote them. "In God we trust." "Endowed by their Creator." "One nation under God." The ACLU is working to get rid of those too.

After the 1915 San Diego World's Fair in Balboa Park, the Santa Fe Railroad donated its Pueblo Indian village to local Boy Scouts with approval by the city council. For twenty-five years, the Scouts used the Indian village as a headquarters and recreation site free of charge. During World War II, the military took possession of Balboa Park, and the Boy Scouts launched their volunteer campaigns to help the war effort from a makeshift headquarters in a local theater.

At the end of the war, the San Diego City Council passed a resolution authorizing the Boy Scouts to take charge of several acres of land in Balboa Park. Through fund-raising and volunteer work, a state-of-the-art swimming pool and a six-hundred-seat outdoor amphitheater were constructed. In 1949, the Boy Scouts Desert Pacific Council headquarters building was completed.

In 1957, parts of Balboa Park remained undeveloped, so the city council agreed to transfer additional property to the Boy Scouts for maintenance and operations. A fifty-year lease was signed with a rental fee of one dollar per year. With nearly sixteen acres of leased land, the Boy Scouts soon launched Camp Balboa.[22]

Today, Camp Balboa accommodates up to three hundred campers and offers a variety of year-round programs. Each year, twelve thousand Boy Scouts take part in day camps, weekend camps, and merit badge classes.[23] According to David Hodges, field director for the Desert Pacific Boy Scout Council, "The park is used by everybody. We run this portion of the park. We reserve it for outside groups and anybody's welcome to use it. We do all the upkeep of the property here, and we lease it from the city. All the maintenance, all the expenses, the landscaping, everything we take care of."[24]

A year after the Balboa Park ruling, Judge Jones made a second ruling in the case of San Diego's Fiesta Island, where the Scouts operated an aquatics center. In an equally vitriolic statement, Jones evicted the Scouts from the facility in which they had invested $2 million since 1987.

Interestingly, a variety of other groups use Balboa Park and Fiesta Island. The week before Judge Jones's Balboa Park ruling, for example, the two-day San Diego Lesbian, Gay, Bisexual, Transgender Pride Festival was held at the park.[25] The Boy Scouts have spent millions of dollars developing and maintaining Balboa Park over the years, without burden to the city and its taxpayers. Furthermore, the city has existing property use partnerships with other "religious organizations" such as a Jewish synagogue, a Korean church, the Girl Scouts, and Boys and Girls Clubs.

Even if San Diego had given preferential treatment to the Boy Scouts, what harm does that do society? Once, the Boy Scouts working with city hall was a common courtesy. Today, such treatment is viewed by the ACLU and judges like Napoleon Jones as though the city had given special privileges to the KKK or the Taliban.

The Boy Scouts have contributed to our communities and improved our way of life. It is ironic that the ACLU is questioning the Scouts for practicing character and moral virtue on public lands, while the ACLU is occupying public courthouses around America, pulling down every vestige of decency in sight. There is "over-whelming and uncontradicted" evidence that the ACLU is destroying America, one Boy Scout camp at a time.

ON OUR LAST NIGHT at Philmont Scout Ranch, we held devotions under remarkably starry skies. We gathered in a clearing near our tent site to cast our gazes heavenward. I could not help but think that God had ordered and placed the stars in the night sky, that He had ordained my standing beneath it all in the midst of young men whose friendship could not be stronger than in the rugged challenges of the outdoors. To summarize the intensity of our adventure in the mountains of New Mexico, I searched for an appropriate Bible verse.

The verse I found was Matthew 11:7; Jesus began to speak to the crowd about John, "What did you go out into the wilderness to see?"

I thought it was a good question to reflect on. What are the Boy Scouts doing out in the wilderness? Having gone there, I'm convinced we went into the wilderness to have our character forged by God and to reflect on how we were serving Him. That's why the Boy Scouts of America exists—not to facilitate my relationship with Jesus Christ or interpret the Bible for me—but to demand that my duty to God be foremost in all I do, on my honor.

We went into the wilderness to sit at the base of a mountain, to climb atop a rocky crag, or to endure the changes of the weather. And when we emerged from God's creation, we knew that being a Boy Scout is a spiritual commitment.

CHAPTER 12

★★

Boy Scouts and Churches

In June 2003, Rev. Darren Squires began using his church bulletin board at Socastee Freewill Baptist Church along South Carolina's Highway 707 to express support for the Boy Scouts and their membership standards prohibiting homosexual members and leaders. The sign read, "God bless the Boy Scouts for their stand against homosexuality in the Scouts."

Local anti-Scout activists criticized the church for its stand on behalf of the Boy Scouts. Carol Reeder of the Myrtle Beach, South Carolina, Parents, Families, and Friends of Lesbians and Gays said, "It doesn't make any sense. . . . they believe homosexuality is a sin."[1] It is true that the Socastee Freewill Baptist Church believes homosexuality is a sin, as do all Bible-believing churches.

Dr. Jay Mechling claimed there is an "increasing influence of the religious right in the national offices of the Boy Scouts."[2] And in his book *Scout's Honor,* Peter Applebome of the *New York Times* points to Boy Scouts' affiliations with conservative churches as evidence the Scouts have become a key component of the Religious Right. The Scouts, he writes, have "come to be dominated by religious groups and the conservative voices of the nation's culture wars. Once the Scouts sat square in the middle of a relatively homogeneous civic culture. Now, if there is a middle, the Scouts don't seem to know how to find it."[3]

Applebome is correct that the Scouts were once in the main-stream of a "homogeneous civic culture." What Applebome seems to ignore is that the culture itself has moved decidedly leftward. The Scouts have been fairly consistent in their views on life and their associations with religious groups—the Scouts haven't moved to the right, but the middle has moved to the left.

Even in an age when political correctness has taken over many churches, most any denomination and sect, liberal or conservative, would seem to be a natural ally with the Boy Scouts. Regardless how fundamental or watered-down a particular church is, the idea that an individual is obligated to love God first and his neighbor second remains nearly universal in American churches. An organization like the Boy Scouts that not only begins its oath with words about "duty to God and country" but that goes out and lives those words, ought to receive, as it has for the most part, the undying partnership of churches of all sizes, colors, and beliefs. Churches have much at stake in the war on the Boy Scouts. The affiliation of church denominations with the BSA has always been a source of strength for both organizations.

Today, churches sponsor the majority of Boy Scout troops. In fact, more than 1.5 million individual Boy Scouts are members of church-sponsored troops, and around 65 percent of Scout units and troops are chartered to a local church or religious organization. Besides the religious patches mentioned in the previous chapter, most of the churches that sponsor Scouting have organizations with the specific task of facilitating and assisting the Boy Scouts of America. For example, the Lutheran Association for Scouters was formed to "encourage Lutheran congregations to use the programs and resources of the Boy Scouts of America as a means of extending their ministry to children, youth and families."[4]

WHEN BADEN-POWELL founded the Scouts in Great Britain, he decreed that troop members should make an effort to attend weekly church services. Baden-Powell believed church was a source of "character instruction" missing in the educational realm of "book instruction."[5]

The founding of the Boy Scouts of America occurred in large part because of the decline of Sunday school around the turn of the last century. It may be assumed, by the nature of the church, that a weakening in the faith and character of the American people was precipitated by a weakening in the church.

At the beginning of American Scouting, progressive Social Gospel churches were among the biggest supporters of the movement. It wasn't that liberal churches had suddenly come upon a liberal religious ally. Actually, liberal churches were forced to turn to Scouting in order to retain young men as members. Through their pursuit of the sissified, watered-down Social Gospel, liberal churches had alienated men, young and old. By 1916, only 40.5 percent of Protestant church members were men, and growth of Sunday schools ceased in the Congregationalist and Episcopal churches. Churches reacted by seeking a "manly Christianity" with new men's fellowship groups and fresh hymns such as "Onward Christian Soldiers."[6]

Attracting boys to church was a monumental task that had significance not only for the churches whose membership rolls were deficient of boys, but for American culture at large that was, for several decades around the turn of the century, plagued by the boy problem.

Rev. John Q. Adams, founder of the American Boys Brigade, said in 1891 that "in recent years, there has been much discussion over the relation of the church to young men. Much less has been said regarding the boys, but any careful observer must have noticed that the trouble begins with them. Soon after the age of twelve, a large number of them drift out of the Sunday School and away from the church. Here is the missing link in our church work."[7] Churches seized on character-building programs as a way to restore the Sunday school and church participation among men.

According to Macleod, "Churches and churchmen formed by far the largest single market for character-building programs because mainline Protestant churches in towns and cities were losing boys in droves." Unfortunately, when churches tried to sponsor Boys Brigades, independent youth groups, athletic teams, and organizations like Knights of Methodism, Knights of King Arthur, Epworth Court of Arthur, Knights Crusaders, Knights of Valor, and Junior Order of Messenger Boys, they often failed.[8] Churches' work with boys tended to be sloppily organized, devoid of practicality, and lacking leadership.

In desperation, mainline churches embraced the Boy Scouts. The Federal Council of Christian Churches, Methodists, Northern Baptists, Episcopalians, Presbyterians, and Congregationalists gave excited endorsements to Scouting.[9] Realizing a bold new opportunity to bring in boys to the church, ministers filled out applications to form new Scout troops and serve as Scoutmasters.[10] In 1912, nearly one in three Scoutmasters was a minister, and by 1924, a survey of city churches found that 46 percent sponsored a Boy Scout troop.[11] And churches triumphed because by 1921, nine of ten Scouts were regular attendees of Sunday school.[12]

James West respected the autonomy of troop-sponsoring churches, and he did everything within reason to give churches "a certain degree of independence." While trying to avoid a particular denomination monopolizing the Boy Scouts, West allowed church troops to set policies of allowing only church families to take part in the troop.[13] He also prohibited sponsoring churches from coercing nonchurched Scouts to attend services and official church activities.[14]

Mainline church leaders came to admire Scouting for its ecumenically religious program. Rev. Franklin D. Elmer, a Northern Baptist preacher, said Scouting gave boys an appreciation of Washington and Lincoln, "of Paul, mission frontiersman," and of Christ, "the Master Scout, whose life may be best interpreted for a boy in terms of observation, service, and the twelve great laws."[15]

Since Scouting had been founded as a somewhat Protestant movement, Catholics were reluctant to join. But following World War I, the National Catholic War Council took an interest in Scouting and decided it would be a positive opportunity for Catholic boys as well. Once the BSA ended exclusively Protestant interdenominational camp services and emphasized its opposition to communism, Catholics everywhere began to join the Boy Scouts.[16]

WHEN THE CATHOLIC CHURCH was rocked by a child sex scandal in the early twenty-first century, pundits used the example of homosexuals in the priesthood to illustrate the dangers of allowing homosexuals in leadership positions in the Boy Scouts.

Case in point is Rev. John Hemstreet. Hemstreet, a Catholic priest and convicted child molester, pleaded guilty to the assault of a ten-year-old boy in 1992, and is today out of prison and president of the Toledo, Ohio, chapter of Parents and Friends of Lesbians and Gays (PFLAG). On the Scouting for All National Day of Protest in 2000, the child molester led his group in picketing Toledo's Scouting office.[17]

Hemstreet explained he is an example of a good Boy Scout leader because he is no longer a child molester and in a way he was giving back to the community by urging the Scouts to accept child molesters as leaders. Columnist Joseph Farah of WorldNetDaily.com wrote that Hemstreet was a revealing representative of his movement because "Some homosexuals want to be around children for one reason—to prey on them."[18]

The Catholic Church is officially intolerant of homosexual deviancy and child sex abuse in its priesthood. In his 1982 treatise about the Boy Scout handbook, Paul Fussell compared the Boy Scouts to the Catholic Church for its ability to adapt to changing times without compromising standards. "The pliability and adaptability of the Scout movement explains its remarkable longevity, its capacity to flourish in a world dramatically different from its founders. Like the Roman Catholic Church, the Scout movement knows the difference between cosmetic and real change, and it happily embraces the one to avoid any truck with the other."[19]

While the Catholic Church has not even come close to condoning homosexual behavior, other church denominations have. And in so doing, they insist on "real change" in the Boy Scouts. A growing number of liberal churches, many of whose membership rolls historically benefited by a charter of a Scout troop, have chosen to drop the Scouts in favor of a new membership demographic: homosexuals.

AFTER ADOPTING a new nondiscrimination policy to include homosexuals, Binkley Memorial Baptist Church in Chapel Hill, North Carolina, told its Boy Scout troop, chartered to the church since 1962, it would have to find a new sponsor and meeting location. Like other groups, the Baptist church gave the troop the option of waiving the homosexual policy and continuing the church's contract. Of course, the Scouts stood firm on the membership rules, and the troop was forced to locate a new home.[20]

Troop 45 of Hanover, New Hampshire, began meeting at the United Church of Christ at Dartmouth College in 1937. Recently, after sixty-five years of troop meetings, church leaders threw Troop 45 out its doors. The Dartmouth church accepted gays and lesbians into membership and ministry and consequently felt it inappropriate to sponsor a Scout troop. The church pastor, the Reverend Carla Bailey, told the Associated Press, "We decided that we could no longer support having this group in the building when we have a strong anti-discrimination policy." Troop chairman Nicholas Collins responded, "They voted to be an open and affirming congregation, but I think it's obvious that they're no longer totally open because they don't want the Boy Scouts there."[21]

Other churches in the United Church of Christ have dealt with the Boy Scouts in a similar manner. Rev. Beverly Duncan and her church council in Taunton, Massachusetts, voted not to renew a Boy Scout charter. She told *United Church News,* "Jesus never said anything about homosexuality." Thus, she concluded, "I feel pretty good about the church having done that."[22]

A 1993 United Church of Christ general synod resolution called on the Boy Scouts to "stop discriminatory practices of prohibiting openly gay" people from the BSA.[23] Then, in July 2003, the United Church of Christ general synod passed a resolution again calling on the Boy Scouts to include homosexuals. "Discrimination against anyone based on sexual orientation is contrary to our understanding of the teachings of Christ," said the resolution.[24]

Still, there was considerable dissent at the 2003 UCC synod. Volunteer Scout leader James Haun from Strasburg, Pennsylvania, spoke on the floor: "I ask you to reconsider your attack on this American institution. Scouting is portrayed as anti-gay and perverted. This must be challenged. This has everything to do with [homosexual] activists enlisting Scouting into their crusade."[25]

Other church denominations and religious groups have announced their opposition to the Boy Scouts or at least their lack of support. In March 2001, the Reverend Charles Miller, executive director of the Evangelical Lutheran Church in America (ELCA) Division for Church in Society sent a memo to ELCA ministers, announcing "support for . . . policies to protect the civil rights of all persons, regardless of their sexual orientation." This, said Miller, "should inform congregational and school discussion concerning their relationship to their Boy Scout troops."[26]

The first conflict between a church denomination and the Boy Scouts occurred in 1985 when the Unitarian Universalist Association protested the BSA for excluding atheist members and leaders. Within a few years, the denomination had extended its condemnation of the Boy Scouts to cover homosexuality, and in 1992, the UUA passed a resolution stating its formal opposition to Scout policies. An early 1990s Unitarian handbook called the Boy Scouts "homophobic."[27] In 1993, the UUA revised its Boy Scout religious patch manual to include language explicitly attacking the Scout oath and law. As a result, the BSA was forced to drop the Unitarian Universalist religious patch from its program.[28]

At its seventy-third general convention, the Episcopal Church adopted a resolution calling on clergy to "encourage the Boy Scouts of America to allow membership to youth and adult leaders irrespective of their sexual orientation" and to "strongly encourage individual churches which charter or host Scout units to open a dialogue with the unit leaders, scouts, and their parents regarding discrimination against youth and leaders on the basis of sexual orientation."[29]

The 2000 Friends general conference stated "disagreement with the Boy Scouts of America's policy to discriminate in its membership against men and women who are homosexuals," but the conference agreed to continue sponsorship of troops.[30]

IT IS FAIR to say American religious groups are divided on the matter of the Boy Scouts. During the course of *BSA v. Dale,* five church denominations filed friend-of-the-court briefings on behalf of Dale, and five filed on behalf of the Boy Scouts.

On behalf of Dale, the United Church of Christ Board for Homeland Ministries, the Religious Action Center of Reform Judaism, the Diocesan Council of the Episcopal Diocese of Newark, and the Unitarian Universalist Association filed briefs. Even the General Board of Church and Society of the United Methodist Church declared that while it would "like to enthusiastically affirm and encourage this continuing partnership of the church and scouting, we cannot due to the Boy Scouts of America's discrimination against gays." Fortunately, the general board does not speak for the general assembly of Scouting's most important church sponsor.[31]

Interestingly, the United Methodist Church Men's Organization was one of the five court petitioners on behalf of the Boy Scouts. The others were the National Catholic Committee on Scouting, the Southern Baptist Convention, the Church of Jesus Christ of Latter-Day Saints, and the Lutheran Church Missouri Synod.[32]

Unconditional support for the Boy Scouts continues from the Catholic, Mormon, and many evangelical and fundamentalist churches, causing critics of Scouting to conclude there is a Religious Right conspiracy to make the Boy Scouts an organ of the Religious Right. But, first, as this book proves, the Scouts' policies are far from being new and were made with good reason. Second, that most churches continue to support the Boy Scouts demonstrates not that there is a conspiracy, but that the Boy Scouts remain closer to the moral values of most Americans than some cultural elites would like us to think. It is estimated that the Boy Scouts would lose a quarter of their members were it to change their policies on homosexuals and atheists, because of their current close affiliation with churches that also oppose homosexuality and atheism.[33]

THERE IS A culture war raging across America, and the Boy Scouts are at the forefront of the battle lines. Whether the larger religious community will have the guts to rise up and defend Scouting will be a strong indicator not only of Scouting's future but of the future of churches in America.

The Boy Scouts have put up a fight to defend the oath and law with a greater steadfastness and sense of purpose than many other once-mighty bastions of character and leadership in America that have now folded to moral relativism. If the church and the family still have the fortitude to resist relativism, they must team with the Boy Scouts more determinedly than ever.

It is time for churches to rally behind the Boy Scouts. But churches must go further than merely sponsoring troops and providing a place to meet. They must actively go to bat for the Scouts in this most intense of culture wars—indeed, in what is more accurately a spiritual war.

CHAPTER 13

★★

Bad Examples

After Woodrow Wilson was elected president in 1912, the Boy Scouts of America were asked to provide volunteers for crowd control and litter control at his March 1913 inauguration. Since Wilson's swearing-in, Boy Scouts in uniform have volunteered at every presidential inaugural ceremony.

The week of Wilson's swearing-in, thousands of members of the Congressional Union also came to Washington, D.C., to demonstrate in the streets for the right of women to vote. The Congressional Union, later known as the National Women's Party, intended to distract the public from the official events by pointing out the lack of women's suffrage.

But all was not well along the suffragist parade route. Crowds became mobs, and militant opponents of suffrage began violent rioting.

But the Boy Scouts were in town.

The Scouts took positions in a row between the crowds and the marchers along Pennsylvania Avenue.[1] Suffragists were shielded from the mob, and Washington police were aided in their quest to control the situation. Newspapers around the country carried the story of the Boy Scouts' good turn on behalf of the suffragists.[2]

BOY SCOUTS may have stood with the suffragists in 1912, but the Boy Scouts of America weren't about to allow girls to join their ranks in 1992. That's when an eight-year-old Florida girl named Margo Mankes decided she wanted to join the Cub Scouts. Or, more likely, her parents wanted her to join the Cub Scouts. In any case, after Margo's application was denied, she and her parents filed a lawsuit against the Boy Scouts of America for denying her membership in the local Cub Scout Pack.[3]

Margo's lawsuit set off a brief series of frivolous court battles between girls and the BSA during the early 1990s. In Quincy, California, a group of girls decided they, too, would like to be members of the Boy Scouts. Their case died after litigation by the ACLU.[4]

In 1995, eleven-year-old Katrina Yeaw applied to join Boy Scout Troop 349 in Northern California. After her application was denied, the National Organization for Women (NOW) filed suit on behalf of Katrina with legal representation by Gloria Allredd. After the initial lawsuit failed, Allredd took the case before the Third District Court of Appeals in Sacramento in July 1997. Again, the court ruled that since Scouting is not a "business organization" under the Unruh Civil Rights Act, it was not discriminating against Katrina. After losing in the appellate court, the case went to the California Supreme Court.[5] Allredd proclaimed, "The Boy Scouts of America stands alone among scouting organizations in English-speaking countries in attempting to defend gender apartheid and gender segregation. We hope the California Supreme Court will not assist them in their campaign to exclude girls from the world's largest youth organization."[6] The California Supreme Court ruled in favor of the Boy Scouts.[7]

In his profile of American Scouting, Peter Applebome dismissed the legitimacy of lawsuits attempting to open the Boy Scouts to girls: "There does seem to be an awfully high definitional hurdle to the argument that the Boy Scouts have to include girls."[8] Even Jay Mechling wrote, "I think adolescent boys probably need a same-sex organization."[9]

Since the failure of the NOW case, little has been said about the absurd idea of girls joining the Boy Scouts of America. Perhaps the reason for this is that the Girl Scouts have thoroughly accommodated themselves to political correctness in order to suit the tastes of radical feminists.

IN THE BEGINNING, the Boy Scout and Girl Scout organizations had nothing to do with one another. At the time Juliette Gordon Low founded the Girl Scouts in 1912, she was responding to a demand that had been filled for boys during the previous couple of years. "If character training and learning citizenship are necessary for boys, how much more important it is that these principles should be instilled into the minds of girls who are destined to be the mothers and guides of the next generation," wrote W. J. Hoxie in the 1913 book *How Girls Can Help Their Country*.[10]

Character development leaders clearly saw a need for a girls' counterpart to the Boy Scouts. Recreation advocate Luther Gulick, a cofounder of the Boy Scouts, also founded a girls' organization in 1912 that came to be known as Camp Fire Girls.[11] Both Girl Scouts and Camp Fire Girls remain separate but major organizations today.

No doubt, Juliette Gordon Low used the new Boy Scouting movement as her primary model for building the Girl Scouts. The purpose, she said, was to "promote the virtues of womanhood by training girls to recognize their obligations to God and country, to prepare for duties devolving upon women in the home, in society and the State, and to guide them in ways conducive to personal honor and the public good."[12] Girl Scouts had ranks, uniforms, and patches and went camping just like the Boy Scouts. For the most part, the Girl Scout code of principles was similar to the Boy Scout oath and law. The Girl Scout promise says, "On my honor, I will try to serve God and my country, to help people at all times, and to live by the Girl Scout law."

Shortly after suing the Boy Scouts of America for discriminating against his atheist sons, James Randall filed a lawsuit against the Girl Scouts of America in November 1992 on behalf of a six-year-old San Diego girl and her atheist father.[13] Randall said requiring Girl Scouts to pledge to "serve God" in the Girl Scout promise was a violation of the First Amendment to the Constitution, despite the fact that like the Boy Scouts, the Girl Scouts are a private organization. Rather than fight the lawsuit and keep its promise, the Girl Scouts broke it with overwhelming support at their 1993 national convention by permitting atheist and agnostic girls to use "words they deem more appropriate" in place of "God."[14]

Girl Scouts executives justified their organization's decision to allow atheist members and leaders by acknowledging the growth of religious and ethnic diversity in America. According to the Associated Press, the *New York Times* reported that in neighborhoods with large minority populations, "the group has had trouble recruiting girls whose religious tradition does not include a Judeo-Christian concept of God."[15]

The words, "On my honor" that precede the words "to serve God" in the Girl Scout promise were, in effect, rendered meaningless.

THE GIRL SCOUTS have become a more accurate reflection of modern culture than the Boy Scouts. The Boy Scouts have thrived by maintaining a Norman Rockwell atmosphere in their activities and a classical ethic in morality. While the Boy Scouts have struggled against the dominant culture since the 1960s, the Girl Scouts have gone along with the flow of political correctness. Nowhere is the tendency to abandon traditional virtue in moral education "more evident," wrote James Davison Hunter in his book *The Death of Character,* "than in the Girl Scouts, particularly as its leadership reconceptualized ideas of obligation toward others and the social world."[16]

In a July 2001 article for *Organizational Trends* magazine titled "Not Your Mother's Girl Scouts," Kathryn Jean Lopez noted the increasing evidence of a radical agenda within the Girl Scouts. "The Girl Scouts of the USA," she wrote, "seem intent on a cookie-cutter approach to shaping a new generation of like-minded women with disdain for the past. Indeed, what has saved Girl Scouts of the U.S.A. from the beleaguered status of the Boy Scouts might be its willingness to accept exactly what the Boy Scouts have publicly rejected—the political and cultural demands of the Left."[17]

Service to others was the prevailing theme of the original Girl Scouts. As with the Boy Scouts' concept of honor discussed in chapter 3, the Girl Scouts established an indelible bond between the girl and her community, nation, and God. "Self-improvement,"

said Hunter, was "framed exclusively in the moral language of
a duty to others, and especially of women's social obligation to
men."[18] In the words of the 1916 Girl Scout handbook:

> The desire to be admired . . . is a tendency inborn
> in the great majority of women. It stands in the way of
> their greatest strength and usefulness, because it takes
> away their real independence and keeps them thinking
> about themselves instead of about others. It is a form of
> bondage which makes them vain and self-conscious and
> renders impossible the truest and happiest companion-
> ship between man and woman friends. . . .
> Our country needs women who are prepared.
> Prepared for what?
> To do their duty.[19]

Similar to the Boy Scout law, the original Girl Scout law included "loyalty." Loyalty was defined in the 1929 Girl Scout handbook: "That she is true to her Country, to the city or village where
she is a citizen, to her family, her friends, her church, her school,
and to those for whom she may work, or who may work for her.
Her belief in them may be the very thing they need the most, and
they must feel that whoever else may fail them, a Girl Scout never
will. And she is not only loyal to people but also to the highest
ideals which she knows."[20]

In the sixtieth year of Girl Scouting, Girl Scout officials surveyed four thousand troops and eighty thousand girls and leaders
to assess their satisfaction with Scouting principles and to "encourage girls to examine and clarify ethical concepts for themselves."[21] As a result of the survey, Girl Scout executives decided to
delete "loyalty" from the Girl Scout law entirely, replacing it with
"I will do my best to be honest and fair."[22] The national organization explained its fears of the "danger of uncritical loyalty" as well
as the "need to learn to make unbiased judgments and to work for
equity and justice."[23]

No doubt, the growing women's liberation movement of the
early 1970s can largely explain the obsolescence of loyalty in the
Girl Scouts.

The 1966 founding of NOW, along with the release of Betty Friedan's landmark book *The Feminine Mystique* a few years earlier, symbolized a radical departure from the traditional brand of feminism championed by the suffragists along Pennsylvania Avenue in 1912. Robert Bork reflected, "Radical feminism is the most destructive and fanatical movement to come down to us from the Sixties."[24] It became clear in the 1970s that the Girl Scouts had totally abandoned the Victorian ethic of Juliette Gordon Low when Betty Friedan was given a seat on the national board of the Girl Scouts of the USA, a position she held until 1982.[25]

Under the influence of radical feminism, the Girl Scouts have long spoken out for Title IX legislation requiring equal opportunity for girls in all sports, be it ballet or football. In fact, a Girl Scouts' resource book encouraged girls to become familiar with Title IX and to ensure that their schools complied with it. If not, said the book, girls should fight for equal access to sports. In 1998–99, the Girl Scouts spent nearly $57,000 in lobbying Congress on issues such as Title IX.[26]

The NOW mission statement epitomized the views of the women's liberation movement: "We reject the current assumptions that a man must carry the sole burden of supporting himself, his wife, and family, and that a woman is automatically entitled to lifelong support by a man upon her marriage, or that marriage, home, and family are primarily the woman's world and responsibility."[27] Feminist leader Catherine MacKinnon went so far as to classify marriage with sexual harassment and prostitution.[28] The feminist agenda, concluded Bork, is "anti-bourgeois, anti-capitalist, anti-family, anti-religion, and anti-intellectual."[29] Radical feminism does not preach disloyalty, but antiloyalty, and thus loyalty was purged from the Girl Scout law in 1972.

Along with the end of loyalty, other changes were made to the Girl Scout law in 1972. That a Girl Scout should be "clean in thought, word, and deed" was challenged on the basis that it failed to express girls' primary need: self-esteem. Thus, the new wording was, "I will do my best to show respect for myself and others through my words and actions."[30]

Self-esteem, the paradigm of a new age, became the central focus of the Girl Scouts and remains so today. Though self-esteem seems to be the obsession of most youth organizations with the notable exception of the Boy Scouts, the Girl Scouts are, according to James Davison Hunter, "the ideal illustration" of that obsession. Rhetoric about service to others has been replaced with fluff about feelings and self-esteem. Consider the 1980 handbook for Cadette and Senior Girl Scouts: "As a Girl Scout, you are challenged to be the best possible person you can be." In order to do this, a girl must "discover more about" herself. "How can you get more in touch with *you*? What are *you* thinking? What are *you* feeling? . . . Put yourself in the center stage of your own ways of feeling, thinking, and acting."[31]

The Girl Scouts launched their four program emphases in the early 1980s, the first of which was "deepening self-awareness" and "developing self-potential." The second goal was "the development of values." Values, said the Girl Scouts, "grow from life experiences. . . . Differences in values do not necessarily mean that certain ones are better or worse than others—they are just different. The ability to understand such differences and to relate them to what you feel and believe in is a part of becoming aware of yourself and others."[32] Instead of right and wrong, good and bad, the Girl Scouts dealt in terms of "values" and assumed for its girls the entire body of relativism that accompanies talk of values and values clarification. Virtue was a dying commodity in the Girl Scouts.

During the 1970s, the Girl Scouts stirred up controversy with their radical program of sex education. By 1975, the program raised issues that conflicted with the role of the family in teaching about sex. One Catholic archdiocese cut off sponsorship of Girl Scout activities, and other churches and organizations have since opposed the Girl Scouts sex education program.

Recent Girl Scouts sex education material contains the words "Some girls have sexual attractions or desires for people of the same sex." The 1997 book *On My Honor: Lesbians Reflect on their Scouting Experience* explained the importance of the Girl Scouts for fostering lesbian relationships. Included in the book are stories and essays about how Girl Scout events were an appropriate place for lesbians to enjoy a meaningful sexual experience, with essays like "All I Really Need to Know about Being a Lesbian I Learned at Girl Scout Camp." The book's writers asserted that approximately one in three adult Girl Scout professionals are lesbian.[33]

Obviously, the Girl Scouts are not a lesbian organization, and girls have had different experiences as Girl Scouts—some good, some bad. But even if the figure about one in three adult professionals being a lesbian is a gross exaggeration, there can be little doubt, given the evidence, that the Girl Scouts are increasingly open to homosexuality.

In summer 2001, Mountain Meadow Girl Scout Camp in New Jersey was advertised as a "feminist camping experience [for] children of lesbian, gay, transgender . . . and other progressive families." Focus on the Family reported that children ages nine to fifteen were required to fill out an application asking name, birth date, medications, and "Gender of camper: male/female/other (please explain)."

Robert Knight, director of the Culture and Family Institute, responded to the Girl Scouts' sponsorship of the homosexual camp. "This camp shows that the Girl Scouts are not only not vigilant about protecting girls from lesbianism, they don't mind if it gets promoted under their aegis and on their property. When the Girl Scouts go out selling cookies, everybody thinks this is for a good cause, and everybody buys Girl Scout cookies. I think most people who buy these cookies would be appalled to know the Girl Scouts are harboring organizations that openly promote homosexuality."[34]

In December 2000, President Clinton welcomed leaders of homosexual organizations to the White House to debut the Girl Scout-promoted film *That's a Family!* The video, produced by Women's Educational Media to educate public schoolchildren about homosexual families, used young children to describe what it is like growing up with two moms or two dads. Girl Scout President Connie Matsui addressed the assembled crowd of homosexual activists at the controversial White House screening, explaining her enthusiasm for the film.[35]

As a result of the screening, more than ten thousand members of the American Family Association sent letters to the Girl Scouts, demanding that Matsui retract her comments or resign from her position.[36] The Girl Scouts leadership compromised on virtue, but it wasn't about to give up on homosexuality.

IN ANOTHER ARTICLE by Kathryn Jean Lopez profiling the Girl Scouts for *National Review* magazine in October 2000, Lopez pointed to Katze Ludeke, a lesbian girl from Minnesota, as an example of the liberated Girl Scout. Instead of wearing a Girl Scout sash, Ludeke wears a bra strap around her shoulder; her choice of footwear is a pair of army boots. Instead of serving the homeless or volunteering for the elderly in pursuit of the Gold Award, Ludeke founded a new organization in her community, Queer Youth Exist.[37] Strangely, according to the *Saint Paul Pioneer Press,* it seems that Ludeke fits right into the Girl Scout program.

By most people's standards, Ludeke would seem to be an angry young lady. She's far from being cheerful about life. But like being loyal and clean, yet another point of the Girl Scout law was eliminated in 1996 when being "cheerful" was "perceived as outdated and unrealistic in the face of adversity." In a 1996 document called "Rewording of the Law," Girl Scout executives justified the death of cheerfulness by saying that the "fundamental principles of the Movement" remained the same, but it was necessary to reword those principles in "language meaningful both to today's girls and to those who will become members in the decades ahead." Such reasoning is a far cry from the 1913 Girl Scout handbook, which said it is necessary to be cheerful "under all circumstances," and the 1920 handbook: "There is so much real, unavoidable suffering and sorrow in the world that nobody has any right to add to them unnecessarily, and 'as cheerful as a Girl Scout' ought to become a proverb." By the 1980s, cheerfulness simply was defined in Girl Scouting materials as an emotion whereby a girl might feel good about herself.[38]

And "as cheerful as a Girl Scout" may once have been a proverb, but no longer.

INCREASINGLY, the Girl Scouts have become aligned with the proabortion movement. In 2004, the Girl Scouts Bluebonnet Council of Waco, Texas, bestowed on Planned Parenthood chief executive Pam Smallwood the title Woman of the Year. A Texas Christian radio station urged listeners to boycott Girl Scout cookie sales because of the Girl Scouts' close dealings with Planned Parenthood. Parents of nine Girl Scouts in Crawford, Texas, announced their daughters would be leaving the Girl Scouts of the USA. Pam Smallwood is "not who I want as a role model for my daughter," announced the mother of a ten-year-old Girl Scout who apparently broke into tears on learning of Smallwood's lethal occupation. "I have to make a stand or there's no telling what else would happen," another mother said.[39]

On March 5, 2004, Girl Scouts chief executive Kathy Cloninger announced on the NBC *Today Show* that local Girl Scout councils are free to engage in partnerships with Planned Parenthood. Following Cloninger's revelation, Jim Sedlak of the American Life League made phone calls to the 315 Girl Scouts councils nationwide to ask their confirmation or denial of relationships with Planned Parenthood. Sedlak reported on his findings: "Of the councils that responded to our questions, 26 percent have relationships with Planned Parenthood." Most local councils refused to respond to American Life League's inquiry, indicating that the percentage could be far higher than 26 percent.[40]

Kathryn Kristoff of Plymouth, Michigan, wrote to me recounting her experience as a Girl Scout mother who discovered that a local Girl Scout leadership manual gave Junior Girl Scout troops, ages nine to twelve, the option of visiting Planned Parenthood to learn about health issues at a "puberty workshop." "Needless to say, we were stunned and realized that we could no longer participate in Girl Scouts," wrote Kristoff. A year later, local mothers founded the first American Heritage Girls troop in Michigan. Kristoff tells people the American Heritage Girls is a "Christian version of the Girl Scouts."[41]

Indeed, American Heritage Girls is a Christian organization, but it is not beholden to a particular doctrinal statement. It is nondenominational, meetings open in prayer, and it probably looks more like the original Girl Scouts of 1912 than the Girl Scouts do.

After the Girl Scouts of the USA decided in 1993 to allow atheists as members and leaders and to make "God" optional in the Girl Scout promise, Patti Garibay, a mother and veteran Girl Scout leader from Cincinnati, tried everything she could to challenge the new policy. In 1995, Garibay realized that the Girl Scouts were not about to give up on political correctness. "The degradation was too deep," she concluded. Not wanting to abandon the next generation of American females, Garibay came up with the idea for American Heritage Girls. "So often it is easier to curse the darkness than to light a candle," she said. But American Heritage Girls "is a candle in our culturally depraved society."[42]

Fortunately, American Heritage Girls is a sound alternative to the Girl Scouts, and it is growing rapidly with nearly one hundred troops and thousands of members nationwide.

THE GIRL SCOUTS and the Boy Scouts could not be more different than they've become concerning values. But across the Atlantic, girls have been included as a part of the United Kingdom Scout Association (UKSA) program in the same troops as boys. In 1990, Scout executives decided to give troops the option of allowing equal access for girls and boys to any of its programs. By 1996, nearly twenty-six thousand girls had joined.[43] Today, in the interest of transition, it is possible for an established troop to refuse to admit girls, but it is not permissible for a coeducational troop to reverse its status back to boys only. Even if the coed troop discovers it cannot work effectively on the boy problem that prompted Baden-Powell to found Scouting the troop may not revert to boys only. By 2000, British Scouting authorities required that all newly formed troops be coed.[44]

The UKSA is the larger of two Scout organizations in Britain. Scouting there split after Baden-Powell died. The smaller organization retains his principles and is known as the Baden-Powell Scout Association.[45] But the primary carrier of the Scouting name is the UK Scout Association.

In a statement of special problems that may arise with the integration of young ladies with young men on camping trips and the like, UKSA administrators said:

> Groups may claim that practical problems, such as the availability of toilet facilities or the recruitment of female leaders, do not allow them to provide effective mixed provision. The Scout Association does NOT require a mixed leader team for a section to offer mixed provision. The Association believes that it is good practice for there to be a mixed leader team, however, the absence of such adult resources does not preclude groups from offering mixed and co-educational Scouting. In the instance of physical building constraints Commissioners should first establish whether these problems have been raised as a cover for opposition to making mixed provision. Where these problems are real, Commissioners should emphasize that these are NOT gender issues but are resource problems.[46]

That's officialese for saying that tenting arrangements, bathroom issues, and other gender differences are simply relics of a time when males dominated society and filled the ranks of Scouting exclusively. Today, everyone is equal.

At an October 1997 meeting of the UKSA executive board, a decision was made to admit homosexuals as troop leaders and members. "Society has changed considerably since 1907," wrote British Scouting executives in their revolutionary "Equal Opportunities Policy Guidelines." "The Scout Association has had to recognize these changes in how we describe what we stand for." The new code included a prohibition of discrimination on the basis of "marital or sexual status" and "political or religious belief."[47]

The *London Telegraph* asked Lord Baden-Powell's grandson, a vice president for the UKSA, to comment on the decision, but he said only that the board had made the decision without his knowledge. Baden-Powell's seventy-nine-year-old daughter, Betty Clay, denounced the decisions and political correctness. "He [Baden-Powell], in his writings to young men, and in his responses to many anxious young men's inquiries, always made it clear that they should do their best to keep themselves clean in thought, word, and deed. . . . They should . . . look on themselves as guardians of their bodies and minds and to do as far they could according to the will of God."[48]

Throughout the country, Scout leaders threatened to resign, and citizens called and wrote letters of complaint. Bill Walker, chairman of the Parliamentary Scout Group, an affiliate of the UKSA, argued, "The Scouting movement is required to accept Christian values and teaching, not trendy, modern views."[49] John Fogg, a UKSA spokesman, defended the actions of the board: "Our policy is firmly that no young person or adult should receive less favorable treatment for their sexuality. . . . We don't think that this should be a cause for concern."[50]

Today, homosexuals are allowed to become Scout leaders without question because "there is no link between homosexuality and pedophilia, and therefore there is no justification for restricting Membership on this basis." Only a brief note at the bottom of the nondiscrimination code clarifies what was clearly considered by executives in discussions of sexual status: "Pedophilia is a bar to any involvement in the Scout Movement."[51]

Aside from pedophilia, sexual relationships are not only tolerated but encouraged in the confines of the English Scouting experience. "It is important for Leaders to help some young people to understand the nature of public and private behaviour, and the need to respect other people's privacy and personal space. When two young people do form an emotional attachment, Leaders should both support their need for some privacy together as well as help them to remember their other friends, who may feel rejected by the couple." Far from the abstinence-based approach of the Boy Scouts of America, British Scouts encourage Scout leaders to discuss "sexual behavior and practices" and "contraception" with their troop members. The only significant restrictions placed on troop leaders are mandatory abidance by the new age-of-consent laws (age sixteen) passed by Parliament and to avoid allowing "relationships between young people at different stages of sexual development."[52]

Even an anything-goes approach is used for Scouting leaders to deal with radical political activism dragged into the Scouting program by participants.

"Some young people voice extreme political attitudes in an attempt to shock those they are with. While these attitudes can be challenged, leaders should be aware that this type of inappropriate behaviour can be a way adolescents test systems in order to make sense of them."[53]

If that is not ample cause for concern in England, Americans must at least take note. Since the UKSA decided to ally itself with the homosexual movement, Scouting membership in England has dropped by close to twenty percent. From 1997 to 2003, youth membership had fallen from 500,000 to 370,000.[54]

For radical homosexual pressure groups, allowing homosexuals in Scouting was a significant victory. The most active group that had pressured the United Kingdom Boy Scout Association into giving in was an organization called Stonewall. Two years after the decision, Stonewall held a major gala in London's Albert Hall to celebrate its accomplishments in the championship of gay rights in Britain. Among the entertainers at the event was the openly gay rock star Elton John. For John's performance, he welcomed six young men of eighteen or nineteen years old onto the stage. Each, wearing an American Cub Scout uniform, performed a striptease with X-rated choreography to the tune of John's song, "It's a Sin."[55]

IN CANADA, too, the old-guard Boy Scouts of Canada are now simply Scouts Canada. By November 1998, the Scouts Canada board of governors decided to admit females, atheists, agnostics, and open homosexuals into troops.[56] The new nondiscrimination code reads: "Scouting is a worldwide, multi cultural movement. We welcome people to membership regardless of gender, race, culture, religious belief, sexual orientation or economic circumstances. Youth members are strongly influenced by the behaviour of adults. We need to be sensitive to the traditions and beliefs of all people and to avoid words or actions which 'put down' anybody."[57] The new policy was enacted immediately.

Despite protest from veteran Scout leaders and supporters, established troops were not allowed to remain all-male groups.[58] But in 1999, Scouts Canada approved the establishment of an all-gay troop.[59]

OF THE 153 Boy Scouting programs around the world, the United States boasts the strongest. It is no coincidence that America is the strongest nation in the world. It sets the standard for nations that offer Scouting for their young people. Many Scouting countries besides England and Canada have given in on the issue of homosexuality and, in some cases, have suffered tremendous losses of membership for it. In other cases, the culture is so numbed to the onslaught of homosexuality that it seems normal for homosexuals to join troops as leaders and members.

Americans must learn the moral trademark of the Boy Scouts that so many in our culture have forgotten. We can also learn from those nations whose Scouting programs look nothing like the Boy Scouts of America.

Because, in effect, those countries, mostly in the West, that have allowed a merger between Scouting and the homosexual movement, are morally decadent. They care little for the legacy of Baden-Powell. They have rejected the Scout oath and law. They are much like the nearly two dozen nations that don't have Scouting programs at all. That list includes Cambodia, China, Cuba, Eritrea, Ethiopia, Guinea, Iran, Kyrgyzstan, Laos, North Korea, Myanmar, Somalia, Turkmenistan, Vietnam, and Zaire.[60] Besides denying the opportunity of Scouting to millions of young men around the world, these countries largely suffer from civil oppression and economic disaster. Some are communist states; others are near anarchy or "in transition." Some are subject to the rule of vile dictators, and most of the citizens of these countries have no clue what economic prosperity is.

Those countries—both those without Scouting and those whose Scouting programs have cast off the oath and law—are without honor; the simple virtues that lead to great national success are gone. And Scouts in Canada, England, and elsewhere and the Girl Scouts in America are not worthy of being called Scouts anymore, for they have rejected the very sense of moral character and duty for which Scouting exists.

And so the Boy Scouts of America best not join those nations that neither know nor desire to know the meaning of honor.

CHAPTER 14

★★

Fighting Back: An Action Plan

I still recall a particular evening walk down the dusty trails of Camp Hahobas my first year as a Boy Scout. My grandpa, a couple of fellow Scouts, and I decided to attend that week's nondenominational worship, so dressed in uniforms, we left our campsite and began the half-mile walk to the Fire Bowl, the large meeting area constructed in a wooded hillside where all campfires were held twice a week. As we approached the Fire Bowl, I noticed for the first time in my several years as a camper at Hahobas a row of carved wooden posts flanking the American Indian totem poles at the entrance.

"Trustworthy."

"Loyal."

"Helpful." And so on, read the posts.

When we passed by the Scout law and were stepping into the Fire Bowl, my grandpa turned to us and said, "You know, if you can keep the Scout law and the Scout oath, you'll live a pretty good life." Characteristic signs of emotion filled his face. We knew he meant it.

It is only in a morally confused nation that character, integrity, and love and duty toward God and country become the grounds for bigotry. When Scouting for All's Scott Cozza called me a bigot during a 2003 debate on a radio talk program, I could not restrain myself from escaping the political correctness that constrains many decent Americans from speaking the truth. "Mr. Cozza, don't you dare call me a bigot," I said.[1] For bigotry at its worst is the lethal hatred of goodness. Bigotry is the warped conscience that can see neither right nor wrong because of the prejudice of the prevailing moral relativism. And bigotry is not the legacy of the Boy Scouts.

But if the Boy Scouts are not shielded with the collective strength of tens of millions of decent Americans who care about virtue, strength, and honor, bigotry will become the legacy of the Boy Scouts. For by allowing into their ranks those who unabashedly and unashamedly reject the Scout oath and law, Scouts will be giving into the radical Left.

Fortunately, around the country, millions of Americans do continue to support the Boy Scouts. People are fed up with the war on Scouting, and they're fighting back.

When the openly homosexual mayor of Tempe, Arizona, Neil Guiliano, ejected the Boy Scouts from the city of Tempe employee contribution withholding options in 2000, Guiliano's office was flooded with angry phone calls and e-mails. After intense public pressure from Tempe residents, the city council was forced to reverse the decision.[2]

In Pittsburgh, a wealthy individual read an article stating that Scouting was losing major sources of money. This anonymous person decided to give compensation for the recent losses. He or she sent the Boy Scouts of America a check totaling $1,500,000![3]

Outside fund-raising for the BSA was at an all-time high four months after the *Dale* decision when former CIA director and National Eagle Scout Association president Robert Gates wrote in a letter to the Eagle Scout organization, "Every council is enjoying improved financial support, to the extent that many are making capital improvements in their camps and council service centers for the first time in years. Many councils are now able to begin building endowments or add to existing ones that will enhance programs for years to come."[4]

Despite media reports to the contrary, corporate America continues to provide major funding to the Boy Scouts of America. Katie Zernike of the *New York Times* falsely reported in 2000 that many

companies were cutting off funds to the Scouts.[5] But David Bresnahan of WorldNetDaily.com pointed out that the corporate problem
was highly exaggerated. Wells Fargo Bank did cut off funding in 1992
but restored it by 1998. First Interstate Bank considered a ban in the
early 1990s but never took action against the Scouts. And Chase Manhattan Bank never came close to cutting off funds, stating that to do
so would be harmful to children; it contributes $200,000 annually.
Homosexuals reported that Amica Insurance and Textron Corp. had
boycotted the Scouts; Bresnahan proved the reports false.[6]

Of course, many companies have had to contend with the
United Way slashing funds to the Boy Scouts. Concerned citizens in many parts of the country have sought to raise alternative
sources of financing. When the United Way of Monroe County,
Indiana, cut off funding to the Boy Scouts in 2000, the BSA Hoosier Trails Council was faced with conducting major fund-raising.
Instead, an organization called Advance America stood up to do
its good turn. Advance America raised more than $17,000 and do-
nated it to Hoosier Trails.[7]

When the King County United Way in Washington State severed funding to the Chief Seattle Boy Scout Council in September
2000, talk radio station 570 KVI established a one-day on-air drive
in the Seattle area and raised $167,000 to donate to the Boy Scouts.
Led by talk-show hosts Kirby Wilbur and Peter Weissbach, the
drive not only replaced a substantial amount of money to the local
Scouts but also raised a new crop of Scouting donors.[8]

Gavin Grooms, an activist from Utah, founded Save Our Scouts
in 2000 to raise funds for local Boy Scout councils whose United
Way funding had been severed. Grooms launched a petition on his
Web site, www.saveourscouts.org, to support Boy Scouts shortly
after the *Dale* decision, garnering nearly 240,000 signatures by
early 2004. The goal of Save Our Scouts is "to proclaim the time-
lessness of the scout principles and provide an opportunity for
those who support those principles to effectively defend and support them."[9]

Another grassroots organization called Eagle Scout Rally for
Tradition Foundation was founded in 2000 by a group of Christian

Eagle Scouts to prevent physical and emotional health risks of the homosexual lifestyle among the nation's youth. Eagle Scout Rally director Gary Yinger maintains an informative Web site at www.eaglescoutrally.org.[10]

The American Legion—the Boy Scouts' ninth largest sponsor for seventy-eight thousand Scouts in twenty-five hundred troops and the nation's leading veterans' organization—has rallied strongly behind the Boy Scouts recently. In September 2000, the American Legion passed a resolution at its eighty-second annual national convention in Milwaukee, supporting "the Boy Scouts of America in its efforts to maintain and practice traditional family values with regard to their membership and leadership standards." The resolution was endorsed unanimously. Later, Legion President Ray G. Smith said, "I call on all Americans who believe in the God-given legacies of our founding fathers to stand up for what is good and right and decent—the Boy Scout tradition. I ask all Americans to learn the facts about the assault on scouting and traditional values."[11]

SCOUTING FOR ALL'S Web site features a quote by Margaret Mead that Scout supporters could use, too, for their own purposes: "Never doubt that a small group of committed citizens can change the world. Indeed it is the only thing that ever has."[12] Mead also said for civilization to survive, it needs the effort of volunteer associations "going out and taking social action."[13]

The Boy Scouts of America may be on the defensive now, but they still have strength. This generation of Boy Scouts is surrounded—to borrow a term from the Bible—by a great cloud of witnesses. The fellowship of one hundred million Boy Scouts is a mighty force.

And we must not ignore the culture war, of which the Boy Scouts is perhaps the most salient symbol. In an effort to make a difference, I offer seven suggestions for how you can help fight on the side of the Boy Scouts in the culture war. Janet LaRue of the Family Research Council said, "The Boy Scouts: the best defense is a good offense."[14]

1. Become active in the Boy Scouts

If you are a morally straight adult, there is a place for you in the Boy Scouts of America. Whether you are a doctor, banker, or garbage collector, you can teach your skills as a merit badge counselor. If you want to dedicate time to monitoring the development of young men, become a Scoutmaster. If you want to get involved with the experience of younger children, become involved as a den leader.

Contact your local council to find out how you can start a new troop or den in your community. In a few areas of the country, there is no visible Scouting presence. You can change that by working with a few families and starting a quality organization.

2. Contribute money directly to the Scouts

The key word is *directly*. Don't give through the United Way, especially not if it has cut the Boy Scouts from its allocation budget. The Boy Scouts need money to operate, to provide outdoor learning programs at summer camps, to fund troops in low-income areas, to recruit new youth and adult members, and enhance the programs at Philmont Scout Ranch in New Mexico and Florida National High Adventure Sea Base. And with lawsuits continuing to be filed, to pay hefty legal bills.

3. Avoid doing business with anti-Scout organizations

First, find out if your local United Way and businesses you support have cut their funding to Boy Scouts. If so, withdraw funding that you would give to an organization like the United Way. You can always find competing organizations and businesses if you don't like their message. Instead of giving to the United Way, give directly to the Boy Scouts or other charitable organizations you want to support.

Second, express yourself to the organizations you are avoiding with a polite letter or e-mail telling the reasons why you will not purchase their products or why you will no longer support their causes. Companies will pay attention to your opinion because they don't want to alienate customers.

4. Attend local government meetings

Every school board, city council, and other government body that decided to discriminate against the Boy Scouts did so because of intense pressure from groups advocating the homosexual agenda. In no way is it healthy for a local government to exclude a group as popular as the Scouts. That means the pressure to discriminate was greater than the pressure to allow Scouts to continue use of public facilities.

The most important thing you can do to prevent your city council or school board from leaving the Scouts homeless is to attend as many public meetings as possible. Regular meetings allow citizens to express their concerns in a public comment period. Take advantage of this time and urge your local government to stay pro-Scout, profuture.

5. Contact BSA to express support

This is a crucial step, because the Boy Scouts of America are aware of public opinion. Two of three Americans support the Boy Scouts and their right to hold their own policy. But the pressures to give in are intense! Ensure that the pressures not to give in are more intense. Contact the local Boy Scout council and tell the Scouts you're on their side. Contact the national board of directors as well.

6. Contribute to a pro-Scout legal organization

Several good legal foundations are working hard to help the Boy Scouts of America prevail in court and in public opinion. While they don't compare in number, power, or size to the mighty ACLU and its circle of allies, they are growing and can use your help.

The most important non-BSA legal effort launched in defense of the Boy Scouts has been the Scouting Legal Defense Fund, a project of the American Civil Rights Union. Both were involved in court briefs in the *Dale* case and in the San Diego Balboa Park case, and most importantly, in exposing the United Way for cutting funds to Scouts. The Scouting Legal Defense Fund is directed by former Reagan administration official Robert Carleson, and its advisory committee consists of such prominent Americans as former Attorney General Edwin Meese, legal scholar Robert Bork, Utah Congressman Chris Cannon, Linda Chavez of the Center for Equal Opportunity, Peter Ferrara of Americans for Tax Reform, California Congressman Dana Rohrabacher, and political and social scholar Dr. James Q. Wilson.[15] The Scouting Legal Defense Fund Web site is at www.defendscouting.com.

Why contribute money to a legal group in addition to the Scouts? Because the Boy Scouts themselves can't devote their full time to countering the ACLU. It is necessary for full-time legal groups to do some of the work.

7. *Pray*

Perhaps you're too busy to volunteer with the Scouts. Perhaps you don't have children to enroll in Scouting. Perhaps you're not good at writing letters. Perhaps you aren't physically capable of attending meetings. Perhaps you don't have money to give. There is still one thing anyone and everyone can and should do: Pray.

I do not doubt the power of prayer.

What should you pray for? Pray for America, for America's leaders, for our justice system, and for the family. Pray for the allies of the family, like the Boy Scouts. Ask God to bring a renewal of honor to this nation, so that on that honor Boy Scouts can truly do the duty they are called to do.

I think often of a quote by Thomas Jefferson in which he made a brilliant distinction between when to give in on a matter and when to stand firm. He said, "In matters of fashion, you flow like a river; in matters of principle, you stand like a rock." It may be fashionable to hike without a shirt on a burning-hot day at Philmont Scout Ranch. It may be fashionable to purchase an official Camp Hahobas walking stave. It may be fashionable to design a troop Web site complete with links, photos, and rank information. It even may be fashionable to change the Troop 174 neckerchief color from yellow to blue.

Issues of life and eternity, of God and sexuality, of lifestyle and outlook—these are not matters of fashion. These must be guided by principle.

Pray that principled character remains the legacy of Boy Scouting in America, that never shall anyone have to write a sequel to this book titled "The Death of the Boy Scouts of America." For as long as there are real Boy Scouts, there will be real Americans.

Notes

Introduction

1. Boy Scouts of America, *The Official Handbook for Boys* (1911; repr., Bedford, MA: Applewood Books, 1996), 3–4.

2. "Eagle Scout Challenge," U.S. Scouting Service Project, www.usscouts.org/usscouts/eagle/eaglechallenge.html, 2004.

3. Donald E. Eberly, *The Content of America's Character: Recovering Civic Virtue* (New York: Madison Books, 1995), 72.

4. Robert Bork, *Slouching toward Gomorrah* (New York: Regan Books, 1997), 155.

5. Eberly, 11.

6. Michael Medved, "Saving Childhood," *Imprimis*, vol. 27, no. 9 (February 1998 speech at Hillsdale College Shavano Institute), September 1998, 1.

7. Robert C. Birkby, *The Boy Scout Handbook*, 10th ed. (Irving, TX: Boy Scouts of America, 1990), 562.

8. John Wayne, "What the Scout Law Means to Me," U.S. Scouting Service Project, www.usscouts.org/boyscouts/jwlaw.html, 1979.

9. Ibid.

10. Peter Applebome, *Scout's Honor: A Father's Unlikely Foray into the Woods* (New York: Harcourt Press, 2003), 24.

11. "Spielberg Quits Scouts Post," *San Diego Union-Tribune*, April 17, 2001, A-3.

12. Mary Mostert, "The Scout Law REQUIRES Boy Scouts to discriminate against certain behaviors," www.bannerofliberty.com/OS8-01MQC/8-1-2001.1.html, August 1, 2001.

Chapter 1

1. Melodie Wright, "Scouting: An Elderly Eagle Makes History," *Bremerton Sun*, March 10, 2003, A1.

2. Associated Press, "84-year-old Resumes Quest to Fly Among Eagle Scouts," *Seattle Times*, January 13, 2003, B6.

3. Wright, A1.

4. Erling Olsen in discussion with the author, March 2003.

5. Ibid.

6. Winston Churchill, *Great Contemporaries*, www.pinetreeweb.com/bp-churchill.htm, 1938.

7. Peter Applebome, *Scout's Honor: A Father's Unlikely Foray into the Woods* (New York: Harcourt Press, 2003), 282.

8. "No Merit Badge for Scouts," *Philadelphia Daily News*, June 26, 2003, 15.

9. "Scouting for New Land," *Philadelphia Daily News*, July 1, 2003, 15.

10. Jason Straziuso, "United Way Pulls Funding for Philadelphia-area Boy Scouts Program," Associated Press, August 1, 2003; and David B. Caruso, "Scout Council That Lost Battle to Admit Gays May Also Lose United Way Funding," Associated Press, June 25, 2003.

11. Associated Press, "Boy Scout Council Close to Adopting Anti-bias Policy," December 22, 2003.

12. Dale Keiger, "The Rise and Demise of the American Orphanage," *Johns Hopkins* magazine, www.jhu.edu/~jhumag/496web/orphange.html, April 1996.

13. Mary Ann Gardner, "Celebrating Our Survival: Why May 16 Is Special to Scouting," *Scouter* magazine, www.scouter.com/features/0026.asp, May 3, 1999.

14. Applebome, 152.

15. *Boys' Life*, January 2001, 90th anniversary edition.

16. Boy Scouts of America, "Scouts with Disabilities and Special Needs," www. scouting.org/nav/enter.jsp?s=mc&c=fs, 2004.

17. Robert C. Birkby, *The Boy Scout Handbook*, 10th ed. (Irving, TX: Boy Scouts of America, 1990), 492.

18. "Scouts with Disabilities and Special Needs."

19. Boy Scouts of America, "In Support of Diversity," www.scouting.org/nav/ enter.jsp?s=mc&c=fs, 2000.

20. Heather MacDonald, "Why the Boy Scouts Work," *City Journal*, Winter 2000, vol. 10, no. 1, 14–27.

21. David I. Macleod, *Building Character in the American Boy: The Boy Scouts, YMCA, and Their Forerunners, 1870-1920* (Madison, WI: University of Wisconsin Press, 1983), 213.

22. Ibid., 300.

23. Ibid., 214.

24. Ibid., 217.

25. Boy Scouts of America, "Boy Scouts of America Welcomes Its 100 millionth Member Since Its Founding 90 Years Ago," press release, April 4, 2000.

26. Bill Sloan, "Scouting Vale la Pena!" *Scouting* magazine, www.scouting magazine.org/archives/0109/a-pena.html, September 2001.

27. Rose Marshall, "Background," American Indian Scouting Association, pages. prodigy.net/rose_marshall/page2.htm, 2004, and "American Indian Scouting Association—Purpose," 2001 AISA pages.prodigy.net/rose_marshall.

28. Boy Scouts of America Scoutreach Division, "Scoutreach," www.scouting. org/scoutreach/, 2004.

29. Robert MacDonald, *Sons of the Empire: The Frontier and the Boy Scout Movement, 1890-1918* (Toronto: University of Toronto Press, 1993), 12.

30. Heather MacDonald, "Why the Boy Scouts Work."

31. Michael Gurian, *A Fine Young Man* (New York: Penguin Putnam, 1998), 75.

32. Michael S. Josephson and Wes Hanson, *The Power of Character: Prominent Americans Talk about Life, Family, Work, Values, and More* (San Francisco: Jossey-Bass, 1998), 251.

33. Associated Press, 1973.

34. David Crary, "Year Later, Debate over Boy Scouts, Gays Still Rages," Associated Press, June 24, 2001.

35. Applebome, 251.

36. Patrick Boyle, "Boy Scouts' Holy War over Homosexuals," *Youth Today*, July/ August 2000, 1, 16–18.

37. Sara Rimer, "Boy Scouts under Fire; Ban on Gays Is at Issue," *New York Times*, July 3, 2003, A19.

38. Steve Kipp, "More Than the Scout's Honor at Stake," Focus on the Family, www.family.org/cforum/feature/a0018447.html, November 4, 2001.

39. Greater New York Council BSA, "Nondiscrimination Statement," www.bsa-gnyc.org/statement.htm, 2004.

40. Ken Maguire, "Local Boy Scout Council Takes Another Stand for Diversity," Associated Press, June 10, 2002.

41. Caruso.

Chapter 2

1. Janice Petterchak, *Lone Scout: W. D. Boyce and American Boy Scouting* (Rochester, IL: Legacy Press, 2003), 63–64.

2. Donald E. Eberly, *The Content of America's Character: Recovering Civic Virtue* (New York: Madison Books, 1995), 71.

3. Dr. Jay Mechling, *On My Honor: Boy Scouts and the Making of American Youth* (Chicago: University of Chicago Press, 2001), 189.

4. Eberly, 72.

5. David I. Macleod, *Building Character in the American Boy: The Boy Scouts, YMCA, and Their Forerunners, 1870–1920* (Madison, WI: University of Wisconsin Press, 1983), 40.

6. Michael Kimmel, *Manhood in America: A Cultural History* (New York: Free Press, 1996), 168.

7. Macleod, 36.

8. Kimmel, 170.

9. Macleod, 41.

10. Kimmel, 168.

11. Macleod, 41.

12. Ibid., 30.

13. Kimmel, 167.

14. Macleod, 133–134.

15. David Rosenthal, *The Character Factory: Baden-Powell's Boy Scouts and the Imperatives of Empire* (New York: Pantheon Books, 1986), 3.

16. Ibid.

17. Macleod, 134.

18. Robert MacDonald, *Sons of the Empire: The Frontier and the Boy Scout Movement, 1890–1918* (Toronto: University of Toronto Press, 1993), 5.

19. Tim Jeal, *The Boy Man: The Life of Lord Baden-Powell* (New York: William Morrow and Company, 1990), 377–79, 382–83.

20. Peter Applebome, *Scout's Honor: A Father's Unlikely Foray into the Woods* (New York: Harcourt Press, 2003), 81.

21. Macleod, 134.

22. Rosenthal, 85–86.

23. Ibid., 135.

24. Rosenthal, 6.

25. Ibid., 10.

26. Ibid., 13.

27. Macleod, 130–131, 133.

28. Ibid., 146–147.

29. Ibid., 148.

30. Ibid., 135.

31. Ibid., 154.

32. Macleod, 157.

33. Ibid., 47.

34. Ibid., 49.

35. Applebome, 155.

36. MacDonald, 26.

37. James Q. Wilson, "Incivility and Crime: The Role of Moral Habituation," in Eberly, 70–71.

38. Charles J. Sykes, *A Nation of Victims: The Decay of the American Character* (New York: St. Martin's Press, 1992), 49.

39. Macleod, 296–297.

40. Applebome, 155.

41. Macleod, 296–298.

42. Ibid.

43. Applebome, 37.

44. Macleod, 298.

45. Ibid.

Chapter 3

1. Robert Nisbet, *The Quest for Community: A Study in the Ethics of Order and Freedom* (Oakland, CA: Institute for Contemporary Studies, 1990), 16.

2. Ibid., 12.

3. Peter Applebome, *Scout's Honor: A Father's Unlikely Foray into the Woods* (New York: Harcourt Press, 2003), 76.

4. Charles J. Sykes, *A Nation of Victims: The Decay of the American Character* (New York: St. Martin's Press, 1992), 61.

5. Heather MacDonald, "Why the Boy Scouts Work," *City Journal*, Winter 2000, vol. 10, no. 1, 14–27.

6. David I. Macleod, *Building Character in the American Boy: The Boy Scouts, YMCA, and Their Forerunners, 1870-1920* (Madison, WI: University of Wisconsin Press, 1983), 299.

7. Applebome, 241.

8. Gertrude Himmelfarb, *One Nation, Two Cultures* (New York: Knopf, 1999).

9. MacDonald.

10. Dr. Jay Mechling, *On My Honor: Boy Scouts and the Making of American Youth* (Chicago: University of Chicago Press, 2001), 226.

11. Jay E. Adams, *The Biblical View of Self Esteem, Self Love, and Self Image* (Eugene, OR: Harvest House, 1986), 3.

12. Frank Hearn, *Moral Order and Social Disorder: The American Search for Civil Society* (Hawthorne, NY: Aldine de Gruyter, 1997), 85.

13. Adams, 73.

14. Michael S. Josephson and Wes Hanson, *The Power of Character: Prominent Americans Talk about Life, Family, Work, Values, and More* (San Francisco: Jossey-Bass, 1998), 174.

15. Sharon R. Krause, *Liberalism with Honor* (London: Harvard University Press, 2002), 6.

16. Ibid., 4.

17. Alexis de Tocqueville, *Democracy in America,* ed. D. Winthrop and H. Mansfield (Chicago: University of Chicago Press, 2000), 590.

18. Sykes, 50.

19. Tocqueville, 593.

20. Ibid., 596.

21. Ibid., 599.

22. Ibid., 597.

23. Ibid.

24. Hearn, 85.

25. Krause, xii.

26. Hearn, 86.

27. Lew Rockwell, "Boy Scouts, gay lobby, and compromises," www.worldnet daily.com/news/article.asp?ARTICLE_ID=20328, April 27 2000.

28. Melanie Kirkpatrick, "Rule of Law: Scouts' Honor; This Case Is Not about Gays," *Wall Street Journal,* 2000, A39.

29. Boy Scouts of America, "In Support of Diversity," www.scouting.org/nav/enter.jsp?s=mc&c=fs, 2000.

30. William Ian Miller, *Humiliation and Other Essays on Honor, Social Discomfort, and Violence* (Ithaca, NY: Cornell University Press, 1993), x.

31. Donald E. Eberly, *The Content of America's Character: Recovering Civic Virtue* (New York: Madison Books, 1995), 29.

32. William J. Bennett, "Does Honor Have a Future?" *Imprimis,* February 1998.

Chapter 4

1. William A. Donohue, *The New Freedom: Individualism and Collectivism in the Social Lives of Americans* (New Brunswick, NJ: Transaction Publishers, 1990), 43.

2. Boy Scouts of America, *The Official Handbook for Boys* (1911; repr., Bedford, MA: Applewood Books, 1996), 7.

3. Michael Kimmel, *Manhood in America: A Cultural History* (New York: Free Press, 1996), 169.

4. Christina Hoff Sommers, "Men—It's in Their Nature," *American Enterprise* magazine, September 2003, 5.

5. Ibid.

6. Robert MacDonald, *Sons of the Empire: The Frontier and the Boy Scout Movement, 1890-1918* (Toronto: University of Toronto Press, 1993), 5.

7. John Eldredge, *Wild at Heart* (Nashville, TN: Thomas Nelson, 2003), 83.

8. Sommers, 4.

9. Keith Ervin, "Warm embrace for kids, or merely 'psycho cry fest'?" *Seattle Times.* April 10, 2002, A1.

10. Ibid., 5.

11. Michael Gurian, *A Fine Young Man* (New York: Penguin Putnam, 1998), 74.

12. Eldredge, 87.

13. Gurian, 73.

14. C. S. Lewis, *The Abolition of Man* (New York: Collier MacMillan, 1955), 35.

15. Terrence O. Moore, "Wimps and Barbarians: The Sons of Murphy Brown," *Claremont Review of Books,* Winter 2003.

16. James Q. Wilson, *The Moral Sense* (New York: Free Press, 1993), 165–166.

17. Sommers, 4.

18. Dr. Jay Mechling, *On My Honor: Boy Scouts and the Making of American Youth* (Chicago: University of Chicago Press, 2001), 234.

19. MacDonald, 5.

20. Heather MacDonald, "Why the Boy Scouts Work," *City Journal,* Winter 2000, vol. 10, no. 1, 14–27.

21. Eldredge, 128.

22. Moore.

23. Heather MacDonald, 104.

24. Robert MacDonald, 175.

25. David I. Macleod, *Building Character in the American Boy: The Boy Scouts, YMCA, and Their Forerunners, 1870-1920* (Madison, WI: University of Wisconsin Press, 1983), 110.

26. David Rosenthal, *The Character Factory: Baden-Powell's Boy Scouts and the Imperatives of Empire* (New York: Pantheon Books, 1986), 129.

27. Macleod, 108.

Chapter 5

1. Summary, Hans Zeiger and Matt Hill debate, *Viewpoints Radio* with Lockwood Phillips, WTKF, Atlantic, NC, March 2004.

2. Dr. Jay Mechling, *On My Honor: Boy Scouts and the Making of American Youth* (Chicago: University of Chicago Press, 2001), 207.

3. William A. Donohue, *On the Front Lines of the Culture War: Recent Attacks on the Boy Scouts of America* (Claremont, CA: Claremont Institute, 1993).

4. Todd S. Purdum, "California justices allow Scouts to bar gay and atheist members," *New York Times,* March 24, 1998, A1.

5. Donohue, Sneath quote.

6. American Civil Liberties Union, "CA Supreme Court takes Gay Eagle Scout's Bias Suit," www.archive.aclu.org/news/w010898b.html, January 8, 1998.

7. Mechling, 208.

8. Ibid., 209–210.

9. Ibid., 220.

10. Patrick Boyle, "Boy Scouts' Holy War over Homosexuals," *Youth Today,* July/August 2000, 1, 16–18.

11. William Rehnquist, U.S. chief justice, *Boy Scouts of America and Monmouth Council v. James Dale,* U.S. Supreme Court, no. 99–699, June 28, 2000, Cornell Legal Information Institute, www.supct.law.cornell.edu/supct/html/99-699.ZO.html.

12. Boy Scouts of America, "BSA Board Affirms Traditional Leadership Standards," news release, www.scouting.org/nav/enter.jsp?s=mc&c=fs, February 6, 2002.

13. Sabrina Walters, "Scouts Dump Seven Packs in Oak Park," *Chicago Sun-Times,* January 26, 2001, 18.

14. Robert C. Birkby, *The Boy Scout Handbook,* 11th ed. (Irving, TX: Boy Scouts of America, 1998), 376.

15. Harry V. Jaffa, *Homosexuality and the Natural Law* (Claremont, CA: Claremont Institute, 1990), 8.

16. Larry P. Arnn and Douglas Jeffrey, *Moral Ideas for America* (Claremont, CA: Claremont Institute, 1993), 19.

17. Christopher Wolfe, ed., *Homosexuality and American Public Life* (Dallas, TX: Spence Publishing, 1999), x.

18. Ibid., 105.

19. Rosaline Bush, "The Kinsey Legacy," Concerned Women for America, www.lafalce.com/library/education/1997-10_fv_caitlin.shtml#legacy, October 1997.

20. Judith Reisman, "Kinsey and the Homosexual Revolution," Leadership University, www.leaderu.com/jhs/reisman.html, July 13, 2002.

21. Sex Information and Education Council of the United States, "About SIECUS," www.siecus.org/about/abou0000.html, 2003.

22. Arnn and Jeffrey, 15–16.

23. Ibid.

24. American Psychological Association, Council of Representatives minutes, *American Psychologist, 30* (1975), 633. See also Robert H. Knight, "'Sexual Orientation' and American Culture," Culture and Family Institute, 2001, 4.

25. Bush, xvii.

26. Wolfe, 99.

27. Linda Bowles, "A Change in Thinking," Creators Syndicate, www.townhall.com/columnists/lindabowles/lb20010522.shtml, May 22, 2001.

28. Alfred Cox, M.D., Resolution 414, American Medical Association house of delegates, www.ama-assn.org/ama/upload/mm/hod_d414_rtf.rtf, May 11, 2001.

29. Dale O'Leary, "Gay Teens, the Boy Scouts, and the AMA Policy," National Association for Research and Therapy of Homosexuality, from *Heartbeat News* no. 20, www.narth.com/docs/teensama.html, June 21, 2001.

30. Ibid.

31. Ibid.

Chapter 6

1. Dr. Jay Mechling, *On My Honor: Boy Scouts and the Making of American Youth* (Chicago: University of Chicago Press, 2001).

2. Gregg Shields, e-mail to author, April 6, 2004.

3. Paul Cameron and Kirk Cameron, *Right or Wrong: Should the Boy Scouts Include Homosexuals?* (Colorado Springs, CO: Family Research Institute, 2003), 9.

4. Ibid., 13.

5. Ibid., 15.

6. Ibid.

7. Ibid., 16.

8. Jon Dougherty, "Report: Pedophilia more common among gays," World Net Daily, www.wnd.com/news/article.asp?ARTICLE_ID=27431, April 29, 2002.

9. Timothy J. Dailey, "The Connection between Homosexuality and Child Sexual Abuse," Family Research Council policy paper, issue 247, November–December 2002, 19.

10. Patrick Boyle, *Scout's Honor: Sexual Abuse in America's Most Trusted Institution* (San Francisco: Prima Press, 1994), 32.

11. David M. Bresnahan, "Boy Scouts must defend against 'sexual predators,'" World Net Daily, www.wnd.com/news/article.asp?ARTICLE_ID=13205, August 30, 2000.

12. Dougherty.

13. Boyle, 6.

14. Ibid., 7.

15. Ibid., 70.

16. Boyle, 56.

17. Ibid., 39.

18. Ibid., 57.

19. Ibid., 72.

20. Rosaline Bush, "The Kinsey Legacy," Concerned Women for America, www.lafalce.com/library/education/1997-10_fv_caitlin.shtml#legacy, October 1997.

21. Boyle, 32.

22. Boyle, 67–69.

23. Ibid., 63.

24. Ibid., 315–316.

25. Steve Kipp, "More Than the Scout's Honor at Stake," Focus on the Family, www.family.org/cforum/feature/a0018447.html, November 4, 2001.

26. Cameron and Cameron, 21.

27. Dailey, 19.

28. Boyle, 241.

29. Ibid., 256.

30. Ibid., 258.

31. Ibid., 261.

32. Ibid., 278.

33. Ibid., 334.

34. Ibid., 272.

35. Ibid., 273.

36. Ibid., 275.

37. Ibid., 287.

38. Ibid., 304.

39. Ibid., 309.

40. Peter Applebome, *Scout's Honor: A Father's Unlikely Foray into the Woods* (New York: Harcourt Press, 2003), 244–245.

41. John M. Hubbell, "Gays Reaffirmed as Big Brothers, Sisters," *San Francisco Chronicle,* August 16, 2002, A2.

42. Cameron and Cameron, 22.

43. Matthew Lum, "Religious Right Attacks Big Brothers Big Sisters for Reaffirming Commitment to Diversity," Texas Triangle, www.txtriangle.com/archive/1042/topstories.htm, July 26, 2002.

44. Lynn Vincent, "Brothers up in Arms," *World* magazine, www.worldmag.com/world/issue/10-26-02/cover_1.asp, October 26, 2002.

Chapter 7

1. Jane Meredith Adams, "Unwelcome at the Campfire," *Boston Globe,* www.bsa-discrimination.org/html/forgotten_scouts.html, November 12, 1991.

2. David I. Macleod, *Building Character in the American Boy: The Boy Scouts, YMCA, and Their Forerunners, 1870-1920* (Madison, WI: University of Wisconsin Press, 1983), 204.

3. Heather MacDonald, "Why the Boy Scouts Work," *City Journal,* Winter 2000, vol. 10, no. 1, 14–27.

4. Matthew Cella, "Amendment Undoes Ruling Restoring Gay Scout Leaders," *Washington Times,* September 27, 2001.

5. Macleod, 182–183.

6. William A. Donohue, *On the Front Lines of the Culture War: Recent Attacks on the Boy Scouts of America* (Claremont, CA: Claremont Institute, 1993).

7. William A. Donohue, *Twilight of Liberty: The Legacy of the ACLU* (New Brunswick, NJ: Transaction Books, 1994), 134.

8. Erik Meers, "The Model Boy Scout," *The Advocate,* www.advocate.com/html/stories/792/792_dale757.asp, April 14, 1998.

9. Ibid.

10. William Rehnquist, U.S. chief justice, *Boy Scouts of America and Monmouth Council v. James Dale*; U.S. Supreme Court, no. 99–699, June 28, 2000, Cornell Legal Information Institute, www.supct.law.cornell.edu/supct/html/99-699.ZO.html.

11. Judge Patrick McGann, quoted in Chuck Sudetic, "The Struggle for the Soul of the Boy Scouts," *Rolling Stone,* July 6-20, 2000.

12. Lambda Legal Defense Fund, *"Boy Scouts v. Dale:* Case History," www.lambdalegal.org/cgi-bin/iowa/documents/record?record=474, April 21, 2000.

13. Philip Griego. *"Dale v. Boy Scouts of America:* An Amicus Brief," Claremont Institute, www.adnetsolfp2.adnetsol.com/ssl_claremont/dale.cfm, 1999.

14. Deborah T. Portiz, *James Dale v. Boy Scouts of America and Monmouth Council,* New Jersey Supreme Court, A-195/196–197, www.lawlibrary.rutgers.edu/courts/supreme/a-195-97.opn.html, August 4, 1999.

15. Ibid.

16. Donohue, *Twilight of Liberty,* 131–134.

17. Ibid., 133.

18. Richard Sincere, "New Jersey Supreme Court Ruling Threatens Freedom for All—Including Gays," *Wall Street Journal,* August 11, 1999.

19. Joseph Farah, "New Jersey's fascist court," World Net Daily, www.world netdaily.com/news/article.asp?ARTICLE_ID=14788, August 6, 1999.

20. Diego Ribadaneira and Michael Paulson, "Groups Push High Court to Reverse Ruling on Scout Leader Case," *Boston Globe,* March 18, 2000, B2.

21. George F. Will, "The Boy Scouts' Unlikely Friends," *Washington Post,* March 26, 2000, B07.

22. American Civil Liberties Union, "U.S. Supreme Court Ruling that Boy Scouts can Discriminate is 'Damaging but Limited,' ACLU says," www.aclu.org/news/2000/n062800b.html, June 28, 2000.

23. Marcia Coyle, "Court hears many voices in one case," *The National Law Journal,* May 1, 2000, A1.

24. Joan Biskupic, "Ex-Scout's day in court," *Washington Post,* April 27, 2000, A03.

25. Linda Greenhouse, "Justices Explore Scouts' Exclusion of Gay Members," *New York Times,* April 27, 2000, A1.

26. David G. Savage, "High Court Struggles to Meld Gay Rights, Scouts' Moral Code," *Milwaukee Journal Sentinel,* April 27, 2000, 01A.

27. Donohue, *Twilight of Liberty,* 132.

28. Rehnquist.

29. John Paul Stevens, *Boy Scouts of America and Monmouth Council v. James Dale,* U.S. Supreme Court, no. 99–699, June 28, 2000, Cornell Legal Information Institute, www.supct.law.cornell.edu/supct/html/99-699.ZD1.html.

30. Rehnquist.

Chapter 8

1. David Crary, "Boy Scouts may lose support after winning battle over Gays," Associated Press, www.warroom.com/scoutsmaylose.htm, June 30, 2000.

2. David France, "Scouts Divided," *Newsweek,* August 6, 2001, 44.

3. Peter Applebome, *Scout's Honor: A Father's Unlikely Foray into the Woods* (New York: Harcourt Press, 2003), 252.

4. People for the Ethical Treatment of Animals, "Ask the Boy Scouts to De-Merit Fishing," www.peta.org/feat/merit/.

5. Catch and Release Foundation, "Our Fishing Philosophy," www.catchand releasefound.org/philosophy.htm, accessed 2005.

6. People for the Ethical Treatment of Animals, www.peta.org/feat/merit/.

7. National Gay and Lesbian Task Force, "Rally calls for change in Boy

Scouts policy; Governor issues letter of support," www.ngltf.org/news/release. cfm?releaseID=308, July 5, 2000.

8. Gary Locke, letter to Robert Raketty, Scouting for All, www.scoutingforall. org/aaic/091901.shtml, August 16, 2001.

9. Matt Nagle and Robert Raketty, "A 'Fireside Chat' with Governor Gary Locke," *Seattle Gay News,* www.sgn.org/2002/01/25/, January 25, 2002.

10. Catherina Hurlburt, "So Much for Tolerance," *Family Voice,* Concerned Women for America, January/February 2001, www.cwfa.org/familyvoice/2001-01/22-27.asp.

11. Jon Dougherty, "Dems and Boy Scouts: 'For the children?'" World Net Daily, www.worldnetdaily.com/news/article.asp?ARTICLE_ID=15911, August 21, 2000.

12. Peter H. Schuck, "Diversity Demands Exclusivity," *The American Lawyer,* September 2000.

13. Valerie Richardson, "Democrats Boo the Boy Scouts of America," *Washington Times,* August 18, 2000.

14. David Bresnahan, "Homosexuals protest 'bigot' Boy Scouts," World Net Daily, www.worldnetdaily.com/news/article.asp?ARTICLE_ID=13202, August 22, 2000.

15. Scouting for All, www.scoutingforall.org, 2004.

16. Steven Cozza, "The Letter that inspired the Scouting for All Movement," Kentucky GLSEN, www.members.tripod.com/glsen_ky/id24.htm, December 27, 1997.

17. Applebome, 284.

18. David M. Bresnahan, "Homosexuals target Boy Scouts," World Net Daily, www.worldnetdaily.com/news/article.asp?ARTICLE_ID=13201, August 21, 2000.

19. Steven Cozza, e-mail to author, December 26, 2001.

20. Bresnahan, "Homosexuals target Boy Scouts."

21. Independent Television Service, "Scout's Honor," www.scouts-honor.com, 2004.

22. Peter LaBarbera, "Taxpayer Funded PBS does hit piece on Scouts," *Culture and Family,* June 13, 2001, www.cultureandfamily.org.

23. Ibid.

24. People for the American Way, "'Scouts Honor' assailed as biased 'propaganda,'" www.pfaw.org/pfaw/general/default.aspx?oid=4158, 2001.

Chapter 9

1. Paula Lavigne Sullivan, "Scouts Survive Funding Vote; United Way: Compromise Delays Cutting Off Funding . . ." *Tacoma News Tribune,* January 27, 2001, B1.

2. Rick Allen, in discussion with the author, June 2003.

3. Doug Dillow, in discussion with the author, June 2003.

4. David I. Macleod, *Building Character in the American Boy: The Boy Scouts, YMCA, and Their Forerunners, 1870–1920* (Madison, WI: University of Wisconsin Press, 1983), 203.

5. Ibid.

6. United Way of America, "United Way History," www.national.unitedway. org/aboutuw/history.cfm, 2004.

7. Macleod, 305.

8. Dr. Jay Mechling, *On My Honor: Boy Scouts and the Making of American Youth* (Chicago: University of Chicago Press, 2001), 208.

9. United Way of the Bay Area, "About Us," www.uwba.org/about_us/about_us.htm, 2004.

10. United Way of the Bay Area, "Frequently Asked Questions," www.theunitedway.org/about_us/faqs.htm#boyscouts, 2004.

11. Gay and Lesbian Alliance Against Defamation, "GLAAD Appalled at Boy Scouts of America's Verbal Gay Bashing," press release, March 6, 1992, www.glaad.org/media/archive_detail.php?id=298&.

12. Ibid.

13. United Way of the Bay Area, "Strategic Partners," www.theunitedway.org/about_us/partners_strategic.htm, 2003.

14. United Way of America, "United Way Funding of Boy Scouts," www.national.unitedway.org/aboutuw/boyscouts.cfm, 2000.

15. United Press International, "Charity Takes Aim at Boy Scouts," www.newsmax.com/articles/?a=2000/7/19/172225, July 20, 2000.

16. Eric Buch, "United Way Broadens Policy Regarding Nondiscrimination," www.unitedwaycm.org/policy.html, February 14, 2001.

17. United Way of America. "United Way Funding of Boy Scouts," www.national.unitedway.org/aboutuw/boyscouts.cfm, 2000.

18. United Way of America, "United Way Funding of Boy Scouts," version 2, www.national.unitedway.org/aboutuwa/pos_bsa.cfm, 2000.

19. Focus on the Family, "Boy Scouts Update," www.family.org/cforum/feature/a0012993.cfm, September 25, 2000.

20. Jim Burns, "Major Donor Dumps United Way for 'Not Being Truthful' on Boy Scouts," Newsmax, www.newsmax.com/archives/articles/2002/8/12/174347.shtml, August 13, 2002.

21. Lucio Guerrero, "United Way, Boy Scouts Part Ways in Chicago," *Chicago Sun-Times,* November 19, 2003, 8; and Andrea Ball, "United Way Ends Support of Boy Scouts," *Austin American-Statesman,* November 13, 2003, A1.

22. Peter LaBarbera, "IFI E-Alert," www.illinoisfamily.org/issuesposting.asp?docID=303, February 4, 2004; and LaBarbera personal correspondence with the author.

23. United Way of New York City, "United Way of New York City is separately incorporated and is independently governed by a local board of community leaders and volunteers," www.unitedwaynyc.org/?id=7; and United Way of America, "Basic Facts about United Way," www.national.unitedway.org/aboutuw/, 2004.

24. Cynthia Round, memo from United Way of America to United Way volunteers and staff, August 1, 2002.

25. Brian Gallagher, letter to Robert Carleson, Scouting Legal Defense Fund, August 7, 2002.

26. Roy Williams, letter to Robert Carleson, Scouting Legal Defense Fund, July 30, 2002.

27. Robert Carleson, letter to Roy Williams, Boy Scouts of America, September 5, 2002.

28. Learning for Life, "Fact Sheet: Celebrate Character," www.learningforlife.org/lfl/about/factsheets/character.html, 2002.

29. Connecticut State Employees' Campaign for Charitable Giving, "Directory of Charitable Organizations," www.state.ct.us/csec/directory/index.html, 2004.

30. Jerry Seper, "High Court Spurns Appeal by Scouts," *Washington Times,* March 9, 2004, A04.

Chapter 10

1. Boy Scouts of America, "2003 Report to the Nation: The Presidents of the United States and the Boy Scouts of America," www.scouting.org/media/report/index.html, 2003.

2. David M. Bresnahan, "Eagle Scouts drop Clinton signature," World Net Daily, www.wnd.com/news/article.asp?ARTICLE_ID=13204, 2000.

3. Albert Gore, letter to Scouting for All, 1999.

4. H. Joseph Hebert, "Interior reviewing whether to end some ties with Boy Scouts," Associated Press, www.nctimes.net/news/090100/ii.html, September 1, 2000.

5. Ibid.

6. Mary Mostert, "Save Our Scouts Launches Petition Campaign that could affect the Election," Banner of Liberty, www.bannerofliberty.com/OS9-00MQC/9-1-2000.1.html, September 1, 2000.

7. David M. Bresnahan, "Bush Defends Boy Scouts," World Net Daily, www.worldnetdaily.com/news/article.asp?ARTICLE_ID=13206, September 1, 2000.

8. Hebert.

9. Catholic World News, "U.S. Gov't Investigating Boy Scouts for Gay Discrimination," www.cwnews.com/news/viewstory.cfm?recnum=13724, August 31, 2000.

10. Associated Press, "Jamborees Not Affected by Gay Issue, Reno says," *New York Times,* September 2, 2000, A20.

11. Jason Pierce, "Bush Calls Scout Values 'America's Values,'" CNS News, www.cnsnews.com/ViewNation.asp?Page=\Nation\archive\200107\NAT20010731b.html, July 31, 2001.

12. George W. Bush, "Videotaped Remarks by the President for Boy Scouts of America National Jamboree," White House, press secretary office, www.whitehouse.gov/news/releases/2001/07/20010730-7.html, July 30, 2001.

13. Mark Sandalow, "Clinton Asked to Step Down as Honorary Head of Scouts" *San Francisco Chronicle,* July 15, 2000, A1.

14. Boy Scouts of America, "2003 Report to the Nation."

15. Heather Brewer, "Woolsey Leads Call for President to Resign as Honorary Head of Boy Scouts," Scouting for All, www.scoutingforall.org/cwoolsey.shtml, July 13, 2000.

16. Congressional Progressive Caucus, "About the Caucus," bernie.house.gov/pc, 2004.

17. Save Our Scouts, "Rep. Woolsey (D-CA) filed bill to Repeal Boy Scout charter," www.saveourscouts.com/hr4892.html, July 2000.

18. Catholic War Veterans, "CWV Membership Eligibility," www.cwv.org/eligible/eligible.htm, 2003.

19. Jewish War Veterans of the United States of America, national constitution, article IV, "Membership," www.jwv.org/membership/elegibility2.html, 1997.

20. Veterans of Foreign Wars, "Eligibility Requirements," www.vfw.org/member/elig1.shtml, 2004.

21. Lynn Woolsey, floor speech on Scouting for All Act, United States House of Representatives, July 19, 2000, *Congressional Record,* p. H6565.

22. Ibid.

23. Steve Buyer, floor speech, "Opposition to H.R. 4982," United States House of Representatives, July 26, 2000, *Congressional Record,* p. H7006.

24. Associated Press, "House Backs Boy Scouts in Vote over Gay Issue," *New York Times,* September 14, 2000, A21.

25. David M. Bresnahan, "Boy Scouts attacked in Congress," World Net Daily, www.worldnetdaily.com/news/article.asp?ARTICLE_ID=13209, September 13, 2000.

26. Michael D. Simpson, "Latest Supreme Court Rulings Raise Questions for Schools," National Education Association News, www.nea.org/neatoday/0009/rights.html, September 2000.

27. David I. Macleod, *Building Character in the American Boy: The Boy Scouts, YMCA, and Their Forerunners, 1870–1920* (Madison WI: University of Wisconsin Press, 1983), 199.

28. Jesse Helms, floor speech on Better Education for Students and Teachers Act, United States Senate, June 14, 2001, *Congressional Record*, p. S6249.

29. Patty Murray, floor speech on Better Education for Students and Teachers Act, United States Senate, June 14, 2001, *Congressional Record*, p. S6251.

30. Jesse Helms, floor speech on Better Education for Students and Teachers Act, United States Senate, June 14, 2001, *Congressional Record*, p. S6265-S6266.

31. "Helms Strikes Again," *Human Events* magazine, June 2001.

32. Michael Jahr, "House Passes Hostettler Amendment Protecting Boy Scouts," press release, September 25, 2001, www.house.gov/hostettler/News/Hostettler-news-2001-09-25-boy-scouts.htm.

33. Concerned Women for America, "House Defends Boy Scouts," www.cwfa.org/articledisplay.asp?id=1087&department=CWA&categoryid=family, September 26, 2001.

34. Dr. Jay Mechling, *On My Honor: Boy Scouts and the Making of American Youth* (Chicago: University of Chicago Press, 2001), 208.

35. Patrick Boyle, "Boy Scouts' Holy War over Homosexuals," *Youth Today,* July/August 2000, 1, 16–18.

36. Nancy Powell, "Chronology as of 10-5-99," www.unitedstatesatheists.org.

37. Cliff Walker, "Nancy Powell's Appearance on the Tom Leykis Show," www.positiveatheism.org/crt/nancy1tom.htm, March 31, 1998.

38. Page Parker, "Scout recruiting was biased, Appeals judges affirm," *The Oregonian,* March 3, 2005, D02.

39. Shaila K. DeWan, "Manhattan School District Withdraws Support for Scouts, Citing Bias," *New York Times,* September 27, 2000.

40. New York Community School Board 15, resolution banning Scouts from use of schools, www.youth.org/loco/PERSONProject/Alerts/States/NewYork/boyscouts3.html, November 21, 2000.

41. Ann Goering, "Public Schools and the Boy Scouts of America," Ratwik, Roszak, and Maloney, P.A., www.ratwiklaw.com/mnschlw2002.html, 2001.

42. Ibid.

43. Judge Donald Middlebrooks, *South Florida Council Boy Scouts of America v. Till,* U.S. District Court South Florida District, www.bsalegal.org/downloads/till_district_court.pdf, 2002.

44. "Minneapolis Schools Chief Announces Ban on BSA at GLSEN Summit," GLSEN press release, October 8, 2000.

45. Pete Winn, "Scouts Dishonored," Focus on the Family, www.family.org, October 19, 2000.

46. Lyle Denniston, "Embattled Scouts Struggle to Maintain Funding, Ideology," *Boston Globe,* September 14, 2003, A12.

47. Linda K. Harris, "City Says Scouts' Use of Land Is in Jeopardy," *Philadelphia Inquirer,* www.philly.com/mld/inquirer/news/local/6788642.htm, September 17, 2003.

48. George F. Will, *The Pursuit of Virtue: And Other Tory Notions* (New York: Simon and Schuster, 1982), 16.

49. Donald E. Eberly, *The Content of America's Character: Recovering Civic Virtue* (New York: Madison Books, 1995), 104.

50. William J. Bennett, *The Devaluing of America* (Nashville, TN: Thomas Nelson, 1994), 253.

51. Albert Bushnell Hart and Herbert Ronald Ferleger, editors, *Theodore Roosevelt Cyclopedia* (Westport, CT: Greenwood Publishing Group, 1989), 354.

52. Heather MacDonald, "Why the Boy Scouts Work," *City Journal*, Winter 2000, vol. 10, no. 1, 14–27.

53. Eberly, 133.

54. World Net Daily, "California Senate Scolds Boy Scouts," www.wnd.com/news/article.asp?ARTICLE_ID=34379, September 2, 2003.

55. Jackie Goldberg, Assembly Concurrent Resolution 89, State of California, April 8, 2003, 99-3.

56. Ibid.

57. State of California, "Bill Documents" Assembly Concurrent Resolution 89, www.leginfo.ca.gov/cgi-bin/postquery?bill_number=acr_89&sess=PREV&house=B&author=goldberg.

58. World Net Daily.

Chapter 11

1. Robert C. Birkby, *The Boy Scout Handbook*, 11th ed. (Irving, TX: Boy Scouts of America, 1998), 94.

2. BSA National Executive Board. "Reaffirmation of the Position of the Boy Scouts of America on Duty to God," U.S. Scouting Service Project, www.usscouts.org/aboutbsa/rpa1991.html, June 12, 1991.

3. Bill Murchison, *Reclaiming Morality in America* (Nashville, TN: Thomas Nelson, 1994), 175.

4. Peter Kreeft, *Back to Virtue: Traditional Moral Wisdom for Modern Moral Confusion* (San Francisco: Ignatius, 1992), 194.

5. Rev. Christopher Lensch, "Post-Modernism: Without Law, 'Without Hope, and Without God in the World,'" *Western Reformed Seminary Journal*, August 1999.

6. Dr. Edward Oliver, "The Post-Modern Opiate of the People," *Western Reformed Seminary Journal*, August 1999.

7. Robert C. Birkby, *The Boy Scout Handbook*, 10th ed. (Irving, TX: Boy Scouts of America, 1990), 624–626.

8. David I. Macleod, *Building Character in the American Boy: The Boy Scouts, YMCA, and Their Forerunners, 1870–1920* (Madison, WI: University of Wisconsin Press, 1983), 176.

9. Dr. Jay Mechling, *On My Honor: Boy Scouts and the Making of American Youth* (Chicago: University of Chicago Press, 2001), 35–36.

10. Annie Laurie Gaylor, "Boy Scouts of America Practices Discrimination," Freedom from Religion Foundation, www.ffrf.org/timely/bsa.php, 2000.

11. Ibid.

12. William J. Federer, *America's God and Country* (Coppell, TX: Fame Publishing, 1994), 613. United States Court of Appeals–7th Circuit; May 17, 1993, *Walsh v. Boy Scouts of America.*

13. Macleod, 177.

14. Todd Monroe Pence, "Not Practicing What You Preach: The Boy Scouts of America's Refusal to Recognize Atheism," www.infidels.org/library/modern/todd_pence/scout.html, 1993.

15. Davan Maharaj, "Oath to God Fight Goes to California's Top Court," *Los Angeles Times,* December 23, 1997, A8.

16. Ibid.

17. Mechling, 37.

18. Ibid., 210.

19. Ray Huard and Marisa Taylor, "Scouts' Balboa Park Lease Ruled Unconstitutional," *San Diego Union-Tribune,* August 1, 2003, A1.

20. Ibid.

21. Judge Napoleon Jones, *Barnes-Wallace v. Boy Scouts of America,* U.S. District Court Southern District of California, July 31, 2003, p. 11

22. Richard Amero, "The Boy Scouts of America and Balboa Park," Glimpses into San Diego's Past, members.cox.net/ramero/scouts.htm, August 30, 2000.

23. Deroy Murdock, "No Boy Scouts," *National Review* Online, www.nationalreview.com/murdock/murdock200402270920.asp, February 27, 2004.

24. David Bresnahan, "Homosexuals protest 'bigot' Boy Scouts," World Net Daily, www.worldnetdaily.com/news/article.asp?ARTICLE_ID=13202, August 22, 2000.

25. Howard Menzer, "Scouting for All Information Booth at San Diego Gay Pride," San Diego Scouting for All, sdscoutingforall.org/pr62003.html, July 2003.

Chapter 12

1. Kenneth Gailliard, "Church's Sign on Scouts Policy Gets Support, Criticism," *Myrtle Beach Sun News,* June 18, 2003, C2.

2. Dr. Jay Mechling, *On My Honor: Boy Scouts and the Making of American Youth* (Chicago: University of Chicago Press, 2001), 219.

3. Peter Applebome, *Scout's Honor: A Father's Unlikely Foray into the Woods* (New York: Harcourt Press, 2003), 240.

4. Patrick Boyle, "Boy Scouts' Holy War over Homosexuals" *Youth Today,* July/August 2000, 1, 16–18.

5. David I. Macleod, *Building Character in the American Boy: The Boy Scouts, YMCA, and Their Forerunners, 1870–1920* (Madison, WI: University of Wisconsin Press, 1983), 137.

6. Ibid., 48.

7. Ibid., 42.

8. Ibid., 188–189.

9. Ibid., 192.

10. Ibid., 172.

11. Ibid., 190.

12. Ibid., 192.

13. Ibid., 162–163.

14. Ibid., 176.

15. Ibid., 197.

16. Ibid., 197–198.

17. Joseph Farah, "Who's afraid of the Boy Scouts?" World Net Daily, www.worldnetdaily.com/news/article.asp?ARTICLE_ID=15032, August 23, 2000.

18. Ibid.

19. Applebome, 159.

20. People for the American Way, "Chapel Hill: Community responds to Scouts' discriminatory policy," www.pfaw.org/pfaw/general/default.aspx?oid=2449, April 2001.

21. Associated Press, "Church Ousts Boy Scout Troop over Homosexual Issue," *Boston Globe,* March 9, 2002, A5.

22. W. Evan Golder, "Boy Scout policy threatens church ties," United Church News, www.ucc.org/ucnews/apr01/scouts.htm, April 2001.

23. Boyle, 1, 16–18.

24. United Church of Christ, "The United Church of Christ and the Boy Scouts of America," resolution, www.ucc.org/synod/resolutions/scouts24.pdf, July 2003.

25. Tim Kershner, "UCC urges Boy Scouts to change policies excluding openly gay members," United Church News, www.ucc.org/synod/news/tue-scouts.htm, July 13, 2003.

26. Rev. Charles Miller, "ELCA Policy and the Boy Scouts," Evangelical Lutheran Church in America Division for Church in Society, www.elca.org/dcs/elcapolicy.boyscouts.html, March 15, 2001.

27. Boyle, 1, 16–18.

28. John Hurley, "The UUA and the Boy Scouts of America: A Continuing Struggle for Inclusiveness" www.uua.org/news/scouts, 2002.

29. Episcopal Church, *Journal of the 2000 General Convention* (New York: General Convention, 2001), 338.

30. General Conference of the Religious Society of Friends, "Minute on Scouting," www.fgcquaker.org/library/fgc-news/scoutingminute.html.

31. Erik Alsgaard, "United Methodist General Board of Church and Society Decries Supreme Court Decision Allowing Discrimination by Boy Scouts of America," www.scoutingforall.org/news/static/umc.html, June 28, 2000.

32. Mark Tooley, "Homosexual Activists Are after the Boy Scouts Again," *Insight on the News,* May 17, 1999.

33. Applebome, 247.

Chapter 13

1. David I. Macleod, *Building Character in the American Boy: The Boy Scouts, YMCA, and Their Forerunners, 1870–1920* (Madison, WI: University of Wisconsin Press, 1983), 174.

2. "Parade Protest Arouses Senate," *New York Times,* March 5, 1913, 8.

3. William Raspberry, "There Are Gender Differences Worth Celebrating," *Atlanta Journal-Constitution,* June 28, 1991, A13.

4. William A. Donohue, *On the Front Lines of the Culture War: Recent Attacks on the Boy Scouts of America* (Claremont, CA: Claremont Institute, 1993).

5. BSA Discrimination, "Girls in BSA: Katrina Yeaw," www.bsa-discrimination.org/html/Yeaw-Top.html, 2005.

6. Kathleen Parker, "Scouting new absurdities in gender war," *Tampa Tribune,* June 7, 1997, 12.

7. BSA Discrimination, "Girls in BSA."

8. Peter Applebome, *Scout's Honor: A Father's Unlikely Foray into the Woods* (New York: Harcourt Press, 2003), 240.

9. Dr. Jay Mechling, *On My Honor: Boy Scouts and the Making of American Youth* (Chicago: University of Chicago Press, 2001), 232.

10. James Davison Hunter, *The Death of Character* (New York: Basic Books, 2000), 58.

11. Macleod, 51.

12. Hunter, 58.

13. Girl Scouts of the USA, "The Girl Scout Promise and Law," www.girlscouts. org/program/promiselaw.html, 2004.

14. Mechling, 37.

15. Ibid., Associated Press, "Girl Scouts Allow for Religious Diversity in Pledge," *New York Times,* October 25, 1993, A16.

16. Hunter, 71.

17. Kathryn Jean Lopez, "Not Your Mother's Girl Scouts," *Organizational Trends,* July 2001.

18. Hunter, 102.

19. Ibid.

20. Ibid., 72.

21. Ibid., 73.

22. Kathryn Jean Lopez, "The Cookie Crumbles: The Girl Scouts Go PC," *National Review,* www.nationalreview.com/23oct00/lopez102300.shtml, October 23, 2000.

23. Hunter, 72.

24. Robert Bork, *Slouching toward Gomorrah* (New York: Regan Books, 1997), 193.

25. Lopez, "Not Your Mother's Girl Scouts."

26. Lopez, "The Cookie Crumbles."

27. Betty Friedan and Pauli Murray, Statement of Purpose, National Organization for Women, www.now.org/history/purpos66.html, 1966.

28. John Murrin, et al. *Equality, Liberty, Power* (Orlando, FL: Harcourt Brace, 1999).

29. Bork, 201.

30. Hunter, 73.

31. Ibid., 101–103.

32. Ibid., 103–104.

33. Lopez, "The Cookie Crumbles."

34. Joyce Howard Price, "Camp Recruits Children of Lesbians," *Washington Times,* July 12, 2001.

35. "PTA Endorses Pro-Homosexual Video," *American Family Association Journal,* February 2001.

36. GLSEN action alert, "Girl Scouts Attacked for Inclusion of Lesbians and Gays," May 25, 2001.

37. Lopez, "The Cookie Crumbles."

38. Hunter, 103–104.

39. Jesse Milligan, "Girl Scout Cookie Boycott Urged; Anti-Abortion Group Says Scouts Support Planned Parenthood," *Fort Worth Star-Telegram,* February 21, 2004, A39.

40. Jim Sedlak, "Exposed: Girl Scout Councils have relationship with Planned Parenthood," American Life League, www.all.org/hp8.htm, April 12, 2004.

41. Kathryn Kristoff, personal correspondence with the author.

42. Patti Garibay, personal correspondence with the author.

43. UK Scout Association, "Scouts plan to recruit more girls," www.scoutbase. org.uk/library/hqdocs/headline/960606ab.htm, June 6, 1996.

44. UK Scout Association, "Equal Opportunities Policy," www.scoutbase.org. uk/library/hqdocs/eqopps/index.htm, 2000.

45. Larry P. Arnn, *"The ACLU vs. the Boy Scouts,"* Claremont Institute, adnetsolfp2. adnetsol.com/ssl_claremont/Scouts_vs_ACLU.cfm#Larry%20P.%20Arnn, 1997.

46. UK Scout Association, "Equal Opportunities Policy Guidelines," www.scout-base.org.uk/library/hqdocs/eqopps/eqopps.pdf, 2000.

47. UK Scout Association, "Equal Opportunities Policy."

48. Simon Midgley, "No gay scouts, founder's daughter says," *Ottawa Citizen,* March 24, 1997, A1.

49. Lindda Jackson, "Scouts admit gays; Baden-Powells outraged," *Electronic Telegraph,* March 23, 1997, at www.bsa-discrimination.org/html/uksa-media.html.

50. "Be Prepared: Bigots on the Loose," *The Guardian,* March 25, 1997, 17.

51. UK Scout Association, "Equal Opportunities Policy Guidelines."

52. Ibid.

53. Ibid.

54. www.scoutbase.org.uk/library/hqdocs/annrpt/1997-98.htm#part3, 1996-1997; www.scoutbase.org.uk/library/hqdocs/tpoints/tp-69.htm, November 2001; and www.scoutbase.org.uk/library/hqdocs/tpoints/tp-77.htm, October 2003.

55. Paul Kelso, "Camp Routine by Sir Elton Offends Scouts," *The Guardian,* December 1, 1999, 11.

56. Darrell Bricker, "Angus Reid survey confirms Scouting is a vibrant organization with very satisfied members!" Scouts Canada, www.scouts.ca/inside. asp?cmPageID=260, February 22, 1999.

57. Scouts Canada, "Scouts Canada: Duty of Care," www.scouts.ca/media/documents/dutyofcare.pdf, February 2001.

58. Scouts Canada Prince Rupert District Council, "Scouts Canada Co-Educational Scouting," www.citytel.net/scouts/newsevents/coed%20scouting. htm#One, October 16, 1999.

59. Patrick Boyle, "Boy Scouts' Holy War over Homosexuals," *Youth Today,* July/August 2000.

60. World Organization of the Scout Movement, "National Scout Organizations," www.scout.org/satw/links.shtml, February 11, 2004.

Chapter 14

1. *David Boze Show,* 770 KTTH, Seattle, WA, July 2003.

2. Pete Winn, "Scouts Dishonored," Focus on the Family, www.family.org, October 19, 2000.

3. David Crary, "Year Later, Debate over Boy Scouts, Gays Still Rages," Associated Press, June 24, 2001.

4. "Scouts in a Jam—or Jamboree?" *Christianity Today,* www.christianitytoday. com/ct/2000/012/32.29.html, October 22, 2000.

5. Kate Zernike, "Scouts' Successful Ban on Gays Is Followed by Loss of Support," *New York Times,* August 29, 2000, A1.

6. David M. Bresnahan, "Most Companies supporting Scouts," World Net Daily, www.worldnetdaily.com/news/article.asp?ARTICLE_ID=13207, September 7, 2000.

7. Winn.

8. Alyson Soma, "Radio Active," *The Insider* magazine, vol. 1, no. 3, Fall 2003.

9. Gavin Grooms, "About Save Our Scouts," www.saveourscouts.org/about.html, 2000.

10. Gary Yinger, Eagle Scout Rally for Freedom Foundation, www.eaglescout-rally.org, 2004.

11. American Legion press release, "American Legion Commander Decries Public Broadcasting Attack on Scouts," June 20, 2001.

12. Scouting for All, www.scoutingforall.org.

13. Donald E. Eberly, *The Content of America's Character: Recovering Civic Virtue* (New York: Madison Books, 1995), 40.

14. Janet M. LaRue, "Boy Scouts of America: The Best Defense Is a Good Offense," Family Research Council, *Washington Watch,* www.frc.org, May 2000.

15. Scouting Legal Defense Fund, www.defendscouting.com.